"Niki connects faith and ney with tender rawness and vulnerability. You will leave this book challenged to work through your existing struggles while resting in the peace and love of your ever-present Savior."

Rebekah Lyons, bestselling author and national speaker

"Niki reframes doubt from a fearful warning sign to a by-product of a true relationship. This book is timely, actionable, and a welcome relief."

Myquillyn Smith, *New York Times* bestselling author
of *Welcome Home* and *House Rules*

"This book is, in a word, brilliant. It's the book I wish I'd had when I was a teen, first questioning my faith. It's the book I wish I'd had in my early twenties, when I was no longer convinced of God's existence. And it's the book I need today, even as a sold-out follower of Jesus. I no longer doubt his existence, but I still have plenty of questions for God. I'm guessing you do too. Whether you are a lifelong believer, a seeker of truth, or someone questioning the very foundation of your faith, this book offers you a safe place to be curious—and a reassuring reminder that you are not alone."

Jennifer Dukes Lee, author of *Stuff I'd Only Tell God*,
Growing Slow, and *It's All Under Control*

"I want to press this book into the hands of everyone I love! In her winsome, practical, and empowering book, Niki Hardy reminds us that God is a safe place to land with our questions. As you read, you will feel your shoulders relax as *God, Can We Chat?* reframes our questions as an avenue of intimacy with God rather than a barrier. This book left me more in love with Jesus and more emboldened to come to him with questions I carry in my heart. Thank you, Niki, for penning this important message!"

Nicole Zasowski, licensed marriage and family therapist
and author of *What If It's Wonderful?*

"A must-read! For every one of us who has felt like there *has* to be more to this faith than simply checking boxes, a raging case of good-girl syndrome, and never once questioning anything, Niki Hardy is the wilderness guide we've been waiting for. If you're tired of pretending like you don't have doubts, that the strength of your faith is somehow measured by your refusal to ever once raise your hand and ask hard questions, THIS book is for you. Niki's words—equal parts hilarious best friend and wise observer—have a way of taking you by the hand and inviting you to dig in a little deeper, to look closer, to see what you didn't see before. I cried actual tears of relief as I inhaled the pages of *God, Can We Chat?* If you are finding yourself at a place in life where you have more questions than answers, I know you will too!"

Mary Marantz, bestselling author of *Dirt* and
Underestimated and host of *The Mary Marantz Show*

"I had the privilege of spending time with Niki in person, and it was clear from the start that she is a genuine Christ-follower—real, honest, and a friend you can trust. *God, Can We Chat?* captures that same warmth and authenticity. Within these pages, you'll find a safe space where you're understood and gently guided toward truth, often with a touch of humor. You're going to love this book!"

Monica Swanson, author of *Raising Amazing*
and podcast host

"Doubt grows in the dark and in quiet, but what if we brought our questions into the light? *God, Can We Chat?* gives us a new approach to familiar doubts. In Niki you will find an instant friend who vulnerably shares her questions and personal doubts along with how she learned to lean into them rather than away from them. With a brilliant conversational voice, Niki will lead you on your own unique journey, while highlighting many heroes of the faith who themselves often doubted too. Whether questions are percolating, you're doubting in secret, or you find yourself entirely lost, Niki will walk alongside you, shining a light toward a good God who is with you and waiting for you, questions and all."

Trina McNeilly, author of *Unclutter Your Soul*
and *La La Lovely*

"In *God, Can We Chat?*, Niki Hardy gives us safe space to ask life's most important questions. With her unique wit and wisdom, she provides a three-part framework to normalize doubt, encourage exploration, and ultimately develop our own understanding of faith. Whether you are a believer or skeptic, disciple or doubter, this book is essential reading for growing your relationship with God."

Kathy Izard, author of *Trust the Whisper*, *The Hundred Story Home*, and *The Last Ordinary Hour*

Books by Niki Hardy

Breathe Again
God, Can We Chat?

God, Can We Chat?

A Daringly Honest Guide to Growing Closer to God, One Doubt at a Time

Niki Hardy

Revell

a division of Baker Publishing Group
Grand Rapids, Michigan

Published by Revell
a division of Baker Publishing Group
Grand Rapids, Michigan
RevellBooks.com

Printed in the United States of America

Library of Congress Cataloging-in-Publication Data
Names: Hardy, Niki, 1968– author.
Title: God, can we chat? : a daringly honest guide to growing closer to God, one doubt at a time / Niki Hardy.
Description: Grand Rapids, Michigan : Revell, a division of Baker Publishing Group, [2025] | Includes bibliographical references.
Identifiers: LCCN 2024039375 | ISBN 9780800746216 (paper) | ISBN 9780800746704 (casebound) | ISBN 9781493448609 (ebook)
Subjects: LCSH: Belief and doubt—Religious aspects—Christianity. | Spiritual life—Christianity.
Classification: LCC BT774 .H345 2025 | DDC 211/.4—dc23/eng/20240926
LC record available at https://lccn.loc.gov/2024039375

Some names and details have been changed to protect the privacy of the individuals involved.

The author is represented by Alive Literary Agency, www.aliveliterary.com.

25   26   27   28   29   30   31   7   6   5   4   3   2   1

For James, Sophie, and Emma

When you find yourself at the crossroads
of doubt and faith,
may you discover that it's here where
true intimacy with God begins, not ends.

Doubts are the ants in the pants of faith.
They keep it awake and moving.

—Frederick Buechner

Come to me, all you who are weary and
burdened, and I will give you rest.

—Jesus (Matt. 11:28)

Contents

Foreword

"But how do we know?" I asked, not for the first time. "How can you say for sure that what we have today is the only inspired Word of God?"

As a Bible college freshman, I'd begun wrestling with some of the tenets of my faith. I wasn't doubting Jesus, not really. But I was questioning the religious assumptions that came along with my church upbringing.

These weren't just fleeting thoughts—they burrowed deep into my soul, leaving me restless as I tried to reason my way through a labyrinth of convoluted questions. I worried how my missionary parents, mentors, and church friends back home would react to this personal investigation; indeed, some brushed me off with pat answers, others responded with nervous chuckles and vague reassurances, and still others expressed concern for my eternal salvation.

Thankfully, a handful of my professors didn't flinch at my questions. They didn't try to silence my doubts or offer prepackaged answers. Instead, they created space for me to wonder, to wrestle, to dig deep. They modeled something profoundly freeing: Faith isn't about having all the answers; it's about learning to trust the One who knows all things.

I didn't need certainty. I needed trust.

And here's what I've discovered time and time again: Jesus is trustworthy.

He's been faithful through every storm of doubt and every season of hurt. When I experienced the betrayal of trust by someone close to me, when I learned of corruption among leaders in my local church, when I watched those who claimed to follow Jesus act in ways that seemed more about power than love—through all of that, Jesus never wavered. He has proven himself to be steadfast and true, not because he gave me all the answers but because he offered me himself, his very presence in the midst of the storm.

Jesus is big enough to handle our biggest questions. He is kind enough to hold space for our wondering. And he is patient enough to listen to every sorrow and hurt we carry.

I love the way Jesus describes himself as the Good Shepherd. A good shepherd doesn't abandon the sheep who wander; instead, he goes after them. He calls them by name. He seeks them out, no matter how far they've roamed, and carries them gently back to safety. That's the Jesus I've come to know and trust—the One who meets us in our doubts, our fears, and even our defiance, and leads us home with tenderness and grace.

This is the Jesus that Niki Hardy writes about in *God, Can We Chat?*

If you've ever wondered whether your questions are too big or too messy for God, this book is for you. If you've ever hesitated to bring your raw, unpolished self before him, worried that you might not measure up, let me assure you: Niki knows exactly how you feel. And she writes as someone who has been there—not as an expert handing out answers from a distance but as a fellow traveler who has wrestled with her own doubts and found Jesus to be trustworthy and true.

I've had the privilege of walking alongside Niki as she brought this book to life. I've seen her pour her heart into these chapters with an honesty and vulnerability that is rare and refreshing. Writing a book is never easy, and writing a book like this—one that wrestles with the intersection of faith and doubt—takes a particular kind of courage. Niki has that courage.

I've watched her wrestle with these words, turning them over and over in conversation and on the page, not because she wanted to get them perfect but because she wanted them to be true. I've listened as she prayed for you—the reader—asking God to meet you right where you are, in whatever questions or struggles you're facing. I've worked side by side with her, and I can tell you that she approaches her work as a writer with integrity, thoughtfulness, and care.

Niki is the kind of friend you want on the journey—funny, relatable, and completely unpretentious. She writes with the warmth and wit of someone you'd happily invite over for a cup of tea, and she has a way of making even the hardest topics feel approachable. But more than that, she writes with the wisdom and compassion of someone who has been through the fire and come out the other side clinging to the goodness of God.

In *God, Can We Chat?*, Niki offers what so many of us are longing for: permission to bring our real selves—questions, doubts, messiness, and all—to the real God. She doesn't shy away from the hard stuff, but she also doesn't leave you there. Instead, she gently points you toward Jesus, the Good Shepherd who is always waiting with open arms, right there at the crossroads.

If you've ever felt like your questions might disqualify you from faith, or that your struggles were too big for God, let this book remind you of the truth: Jesus isn't afraid of your questions. He welcomes them. He isn't put off by your doubts. He meets you in them. And he isn't waiting for you to clean yourself up before you come to him. He's ready to embrace you, just as you are, right here, right now.

So lean in. Get honest. Bring your real self to the real God.

And as you do, know that you're in good hands. Niki is a trustworthy guide, and she will walk with you through these pages as a friend who knows the way. But more importantly, you're in the hands of Jesus, the Good Shepherd who knows you by name and loves you more deeply than you can imagine.

He is waiting for you.

With much joy,

Asheritah Ciuciu, Bible teacher and bestselling author
of multiple books, including *Delighting in Jesus*

Hello You

I finally met Jesus over a pasta dinner in a Victorian church with bare brick walls, minutes from Buckingham Palace. A friend had invited me to hear a talk about faith and whether life held meaning, and my curiosity and stomach couldn't resist (she'd mentioned there'd be pasta and cake). Dressed in dark jeans and an even darker T-shirt, the speaker looked normal enough ("normal" equating to trustworthiness in my young, twentysomething brain), so I listened with an open yet curious skepticism. As we took the last bites of our baked ziti and looked longingly at the promised coffee and cake, he reassured us Christianity isn't a religion but a relationship.

Until then, my relationship with God (if you could even call it that) had been tenuous at best. Having gone to church as a family when I was small, if you'd asked me to state my religion, I'd have checked the "Christian" box, not because I knew and loved Jesus but simply because I wasn't Muslim, Hindu, or atheist. I felt spiritual up mountains and believed in something bigger and better than me, which, for lack of another name, I'd labeled "God." In hindsight, I was Christian with a lowercase c—a default setting thanks to my heritage, upbringing, and apathy towards religion in general. But that night I felt as if I'd been reintroduced to an old friend.

Have we met before?

Why does he seem so familiar?

Why do I want to know him so badly?

As dinner ended, Mr. Black Jeans and T smiled and assured the motley bunch of Londoners before him how much God longs for us to know him, and that we're loved and known by him. Everything in me wanted to say yes. This knowing and being known sounded so astoundingly simple yet breathtakingly wondrous. Could this be the unreachable thing I'd strained to connect with, more off than on, over the years? Could this fill the unfillable longing for something more within me? From what I could tell, it would. So with my normal barrage of questions silenced by this new-found desire to be friends with the Creator of the galaxies, I simply whispered, *Yes please, God. I'm in if you'll have me.*

In that moment, relationship, reason, and a thousand questions I'd been happy to park for a while collided.

In that moment, relationship, reason, and a thousand questions I'd been happy to park for a while collided to awaken and fuel a delicate, newborn faith.

Fast-forward thirty years, through massive job shifts, international moves, church planting, burnout, and cancer—not to mention a global pandemic and political, racial, and religious division—and I found myself longing for the willingness of that night to live in peace with my questions, wishing I wasn't such a relentless question asker or black-and-white thinker. The years had knocked what I held true. I was like a tortoise flipped on its back, my faith-feet kicking wildly, failing to find traction. With my faith's tender underbelly exposed, I longed to right myself despite having more unanswerable questions than faith to believe.

Maybe you're there too.

Doubting the faith we once held dear or questioning the God we've always loved and trusted isn't a pleasant place to be, so I'm glad you're here, looking for a safe space to be curious.

We're often told our doubts are our faith's kryptonite—didn't Jesus admonish folks with little to no faith and praise the faith of others? But I've come to realize that doubts hold the potential to be our faith's superpower. When we lean into our questions and allow our doubts to lead us to Jesus, he reassures us that we see only in part (1 Cor. 13:12) and that God's thoughts and ways are higher than ours (Isa. 55:8). Then, like great women and men of faith before us, doubting (far from being a swear word) becomes one of the most faith-building things we can do for ourselves.

I believe God's not as fazed by our doubts as we worry he is or as concerned by them as we are.

I believe it's time more of us know the power our questions hold—not to destroy or weaken our faith but to build and strengthen it. Not to distance us from God but to draw us ever closer.

I believe God loves us—every part of us, including our most honest questions.

I believe it's time for a daringly honest and wonderfully imperfect heart-to-heart with God about it all.

We worry the strength of our faith is limited by the strength of our doubts, or doubting means we're doing something wrong. But I see it differently. What holds our faith back isn't our questions but our unwillingness to dive into the murky unknown. Because it's *there*, in the cloudy waters of life and faith, we discover the untapped power of curiosity to draw us closer to God.

What if by embracing the very things we fear are tearing our faith apart, bringing them in honest conversation to the one we're worried might not be good after all, we find what we're looking for?

Not certainty but relationship. Not answers but the assurance we're loved. Not intellectual satisfaction but intimate connection.

What if the creeping fear that our doubts are chipping away at the faith we hold close isn't the beginning of the end of our faith but the end of the beginning? Here, at the crossroads of doubt and faith, is where true intimacy with God begins, not ends.

If you've come to the intersection of faith, doubt, and skepticism, and you're worried your faith is slipping away (if not totally falling apart), I want to help you find the space, direction, and confidence to not bury your concerns, become bitter, or walk away. Together we'll learn to doubt in conversation *with* God, discover the intimacy and faith you long for, if not the certainty we all assume we need, and find the rest your soul is craving.

Over the years, as a science geek, question asker, and someone who's recently wrestled with all things GodFaithChurch, I've regretted the questions I haven't asked more than the ones I have.

Is your relationship with God worth facing your doubts for?

So let me ask you, is your relationship with God worth facing your doubts for?

Would you like it to be? Because I've discovered it's a relationship leading to a life and faith stronger, deeper, and more alive than we can hope for. Not a life of unwavering belief but unrelenting love.

Over the last year, I've grown more unsure of my faith than I've ever been, yet more sure of God than I could ever hope—and although I'd never wish you a life of doubt, I do pray you grow closer to God each day.

So I created the *God, Can We Chat?* guide to help you reimagine your doubts, unlock their hidden superpower, and help you chat with God about it *all*. My hope is you'll be able to shed any faith-related shame, fear, frustration, fatigue, or apathy you have and embrace the overflowing life of wonder and intimacy with God, come what may.

You simply need a sprinkling of courage, a spoonful of honesty, and a large dash of willingness.

So, are you ready for a daringly honest, wonderfully imperfect, and not terribly holy heart-to-heart with God? I am. Let's do this, together.

Hugs,
Niki
XX

Before You Dive In

Please don't read this book to find out what I have to say or to get to grips with God, the Bible, or your faith. Don't even read it to discover if your faith's worth the struggle or whether you should, like so many others, quietly slide out the side door, grateful for what it's given you but skeptical it has anything more to offer.

From the moment this book was a twinkle in my writer's eye, it's been covered in doubt like a rash. Could I write it? Should I write it? Did God want me to write it? Why didn't I want to write it? Does anyone actually need it? And who on earth am I to try when so many brilliant writers have gone before me?

Was I barking up the wrong book tree?

The irony wasn't lost on me.

There I was, doubting my book about doubt.

The doubter doubting herself and God.

And here I am, about to go to print, still wrestling with the same questions, still holding those fears at bay, trying not to overthink it.

We assume questions need thinking through and in many cases they do. Yet, the thing I've learned about doubts, as we'll talk about later, is they're stubborn and don't always respond to being thought through or intellectualized.

We assume the formula for finding clarity is clear:

$$DOUBTS + THINKING \rightarrow CLARITY$$

Unfortunately, it's not that simple. Doubts and thinking can be like oil and water, refusing to mix. Shaking them together will never create something new. The cloudy emulsion we're left with is simply an illusion where the oil and water break into millions of tiny droplets but remain utterly separate. In the same way, when we attack our doubts with thinking alone, chances are we simply create the illusion of fresh understanding. The reality is, we're left cloudier than before, our souls deflating as the doubts and thinking begin to separate again. The clarity we were hoping for remains stubbornly out of reach.

As Marie Forleo so aptly says, "Clarity comes from engagement, not thought!"[1] So, I've decided to write my way to clarity, believing the answer will come as I do.

The same is true for you, dear reader.

My second encouragement is, for the love of a well-timed cup of tea (preferably served with the perfect dunking biscuit), please don't simply *read* this book. I know you're an intelligent human who's seen, held, and read many wonderful books. I know you can plainly see it is, indeed, a genuine, physical book, with a cover, spine, and words scurrying across every page. So, on the one hand, you're right, it is a book and books are normally for reading. However, this one isn't. Not entirely.

How about this? Imagine that a treasure map, guided devotion, doodles from the covers of your middle school composition books, a hands-on, get-messy, artsy Bible study with your spiritual cheerleader, a faith-boosting retreat, and a good old-fashioned Christian nonfiction book had a baby.

That's this book. Kind of.

Simply put, this isn't a book telling you why your faith is stronger than you think, God is good, and to just have more faith. It's not a book about how to reconstruct your faith in an age of deconstruction, or one with apologetic answers to every doubt and question you've had since you wondered which airline Pontius Pilate flew for. While these kinds of books can be helpful, the point of this book isn't to use deep theology, exegesis, and a large dollop of hope and encouragement to intellectually persuade you of anything.

My goal is to guide you as you reimagine doubt. It's to bust any myths you believe about your questions and what they say about you or your faith. It's to help you talk with God about anything and everything you've been dying to say to him and pause awhile to listen to what he might be saying to *you*. To help us do all that, I've split the book into three parts.

In part 1, as we reimagine our doubts as our faith's superpower rather than its kryptonite, you'll not just hear a bit of my story, but you'll begin to uncover the far more important story that's yours and yours alone. In part 2, we take any myths and fears you have about your questions and what they say about you or your faith, and we exchange them for what's really true. This frees you up to confidently come to God with them and not shy away. Part 3 is where we chat with God, asking your most pressing questions in any order you fancy, with me as your guide.

Along the way, at the end of each chapter, there are questions, prompts, and opportunities to think for a minute and chat with God before ploughing on. And dotted around are a few letters from folks in the Bible to bring it all to life. These interactive sections are for you to stop and *do*. Yes, you could read this book without doing a single activity, telling yourself you'll do them later or they're not your kind of thing (something I've been guilty of). But skipping these sections would be a bit like joining only half the dots in a dot-to-dot picture and wondering why it looks like your three-year-old and Salvador Dali painted an elephant kangaroo.

Why not promise yourself you'll:

Come prayerfully. This isn't about me nattering on for a few chapters and then you going on your merry way, doing your darndest to do what worked for me. This is between you and God. I'm just your guide and cheerleader, and I certainly don't have all the answers. Sorry. He's where the magic happens—in the mystery.

Come with your sleeves rolled up. Some parts of the book can be read snuggled by a fire crackling in the hearth while you empty a tub of chocolate chip cookie dough ice cream. But not all. There's also lots for you to *do*. Things to write, draw, burn, throw, try, fail at, listen to, or question. There are times of silence, screaming, talking, praying. Or some lying on your left side for an entire year while eating muffins baked over burning manure. Just kidding. Ezekiel already had that pleasure (read Ezekiel 4 for the full story). But just like the God we'll encounter as we go, this is a book to interact with, wrestle with, and be challenged by. One I'm hoping will be battered and worn, scribbled in, highlighted, and even thrown around a bit by the time you're done.

Come willing. It can be hard to shake the idea that our faith needs fixing, sorting out, cleaning up, or figuring out. It can be harder still to honestly admit to ourselves and God how we feel about it. So my encouragement is to come willing. Willing to keep your mind and heart open, be curious, dive in, and sit with the discomfort of uncertainty and mystery. Cultivate a willingness to question—yourself, God, me, the church, and even your need for answers. Most of all, come willing to give a conversation with God a go. To start, all you need is to be willing to be willing.

Choose your own adventure. It's tempting to skip ahead to part 3 and the questions you're desperate to ask God, but parts 1 and 2 set us up to get the most out of this last section, so read them in order. However, when you get to part 3, feel free to start with your most pressing questions, hop around as much as you like, and dig in to what matters most to you.

Team up and talk. Hiding away until we have everything figured out feels safe and low-risk. But doubting alone in the dark traps us in the shadows where the lies fester and grow. Inviting friends or your Bible study group to read/do this book together allows you all to share your stories, cheer each other on, and find community and solidarity. You can find a free group discussion guide at GodCanWeChat.com.

Have fun. This isn't meant to feel like work, drudgery, or an assignment. It's supposed to be fun! Why not chat with God in the same places you enjoy catching up with a friend— walking your pooches through the park, sipping iced vanilla lattes in your trendy new neighborhood coffee shop, or with the windows down and tunes cranked on the open road? No need for super spiritual language. Simply chat with him. He can't wait to talk.

PART 1

God, I'm Lost

Learning to Reimagine Doubt

Not until we are lost do we begin
to understand ourselves.

—Henry David Thoreau

I Once Was Found but Now I'm Lost

Standing motionless in the middle of the path, I sighed wearily. Charlie, my Doodle, sniffed the verge with his unwavering, hope-fueled curiosity as other yawning dog walkers politely skirted around us. Tipping my face to the morning sky, I resigned myself to my growing unease and frustrating inability to work things out.

Oblivious to my mood, Charlie tugged on his leash, eager to do his morning business. It was early, not even six, yet the closeness of the day was already too much for this London lass, and the day's under-boob summer sweat had already started to make an appearance.

The truth was, I was lost. Not geographically lost. Charlie and I knew every twist and turn, every patch of hidden poison ivy, and where the laurel's rich green hues shone through the forest's naked winters. The two of us could navigate its narrow curves by just the light of a new crescent moon for his evening constitutional.

Mine was a spiritual lostness. As if doubt and disillusionment had taken up residence and evicted the familiar faith I'd had for so long. Did I still believe in God? Sure. It was everything *else* I couldn't fathom. Thanks to the seismic events of the prior few years, cracks had appeared in my faith and then, as if hit by a log splitter's axe, everything ripped open—leaving me less sure of my faith and more distant from God than ever. Afraid my faith was slipping away, and feeling disheartened and disillusioned, I began to hear worrying tinges of bitterness surface whenever I tried to talk about it.

It was the summer of 2022 and the world was still emerging from two years of global heartbreak and fear. Churches had closed. Churches had stayed open. Christians were divided. An invisible enemy had closed the world down, separating many of us from our favorite people and forcing working parents to hold down full-time jobs from their kitchen tables while homeschooling their kids. Around the world, people were dying in the thousands and no community had escaped. Here in the US, the growing political, cultural, and racial unrest crescendoed into demonstrations and riots against injustice and division.

Living rooms became church sanctuaries as the faithful juggled their morning coffee with cooped-up kids and experienced the strangeness of going to church in an utterly different way.

No one escaped unaffected.

No one emerged unscathed.

Everything had changed.

Maybe it wasn't just the humidity weighing me down. Perhaps it was the growing undercurrent of bewildering doubts, confusion, and niggling apathy towards the church and even God I'd been valiantly ignoring for the last year or so.

One of the weird things about me (of which there are many) is that getting physically lost doesn't faze me. Plop me down in a big bustling city or a wide-open state park, and a few wrong turns add to the magical mystery tour of an adventurous life. Yet feeling emotionally or spiritually lost sends me into a tailspin.

This new sense of bewilderment and disbelief—even shock, shame, sadness, and an undercurrent of resignation—felt untethering, as if someone had snuck down the jetty of my life and untied its mooring, setting me adrift on uncharted waters. It's strange how we can know exactly where we are yet feel utterly lost and alone.

If the things you've endured and what you see around you have chipped or cracked your faith, you're not alone. If you're less sure of your faith and more distant from God than you used to be, welcome. If the questions you've been holding can no longer be soothed or they're wearing you down at a soul level, you're not the exception. Being soul-lost is unsettling, even a wee bit frightening.

> **It's strange how we can know exactly where we are yet feel utterly lost and alone.**

Once home, Charlie panting rhythmically, eager to flop into a hot, happy pile in his usual spot by the sofa, the sound of worship music greeted us. My hubby, Al, was deep in his morning quiet time. Resentfully rolling my eyes with the emotional maturity of a tween—*how did he manage to keep calm and pray on, no matter how jumbled he gets on the inside?*—I headed for a shower, the familiar words of "Amazing Grace" tapping me on my shoulder.

> Amazing grace (how sweet the sound)
> that saved a wretch like me!
> I once was lost, but now I'm found,
> was blind, but now I see.[1]

As I turned the shower to full blast, keen to wash off my mood, the irony hit me. How many times had I sung these words, making them my own? How many times had I thanked God for finding me all those years ago and saving the wretch I was? How often had I smugly believed it was a one-and-done deal and I'd never be lost again?

31

Yet there I stood, the icy jet refusing to refresh me, coming to a very different and more worrying conclusion. Its heaviness pitching me over a cliff, leaving empty dread in its place.

Where once these familiar words were my comfort and testimony, the opposite now felt truer.

I once was found but now I'm lost.

⌁

A therapist might say I bury difficult feelings, but I say I'm simply selective about the ones I choose to hang out with. Not the most emotionally in-tune bunny on the block, I diligently keep 90 percent of my feelings firmly in the happy, skippy, optimistic zone, and I joke I wouldn't know a negative emotion if it came up and introduced itself.

Yet as I stepped out of the shower, I realized that no matter what I did, my nagging, far-from-sunny thoughts and emotions surrounding everything GodFaithChurch had taken hold, multiplied, and gathered momentum. Poised and ready, they threatened to flatten my precious faith, squishing me like Wile E. Coyote under a boulder.

There was fear (is this the beginning of the end of my faith?), shame (I can't tell anyone), guilt (I shouldn't be thinking these things or feeling like this), sadness (I don't want to break up, Lord), disillusionment (why are your people so unkind and unloving?), and disappointment (why haven't you fixed this?) mixed with resentment (after all I've done for you, Lord, and all I've been through) and loneliness (no one knows or understands, and I can't tell anyone).

Was I losing my faith? Was everything I held close crumbling? Could I be subconsciously deconstructing my faith? Was this the beginning of the end? Maybe. I didn't know. Whatever it was it did not feel good.

What Does This Make Me?

The trouble was, I was meant to be a relentless encourager, your spiritual "frentor" (BFF and mentor rolled into one). As an author and speaker helping others love the life they have regardless of circumstances, surely I should have this figured out?

After losing both my mum and then sister to cancer, before being diagnosed with the same disease myself just weeks later, somehow—even amongst the grief, questions, and rants at God—I'd been able to hang on to God and trust him. Buried deep in the rubble of this painful time, I'd somehow found the full, abundant life he has for us all. So I wrote about it.

Readers called my faith "inspiring," "resilient," and "unwavering," not because I didn't question God or get angry with him (I did), but because I always *believed*, no matter what.

Until I didn't. Or at least, I wasn't so sure.

People love my mantra: *With God, life doesn't have to be pain-free to be full.* But I began to worry these words were more fool's gold than eternal treasure. A mere smoke-and-mirrors parlor trick to distract from life's inevitable sleight of hand. Did these doubts and my apathy and anger make me (at best) naive or (at worst) a fraud? A fairground trickster in a white suit?

There were days I doubted I was even a Christian.

Like me, everyone arriving at this crossroads of doubt and faith has a story. Some land here suddenly and shockingly after one almighty blow sends them and their unsuspecting faith careening in front of an eighteen-wheeler. The stillbirth of a long prayed-for miracle baby or the late-night discovery that a twenty-year marriage has been a sham, the husband a fraud.

Others arrive with their faith already worn down. Every pain, hurt, division, condemning word, or un-Jesus-like act done in his name another rip in the fabric of their faith.

That's how it was for me. My faith slowly dying from a thousand paper cuts.

When Church Unravels

As many of our stories do, my church unraveling story began during the pandemic. As the silence of lockdown echoed through empty city streets, the clamor around political divisions, racial injustice, and the escalation of conspiracy theories and misinformation erupted. For my husband and me as church leaders, the health and safety choices we made on behalf of our congregation and staff were weighty and horribly politicized. To gather or not to gather for worship? To require masks or let people choose? Even honoring George Floyd and bringing racial reconciliation further to the forefront of who we were as a church came loaded with political weight.

Couldn't we just love Jesus and people? Couldn't we just "be" and "do" church? Apparently not.

Since the moment a few brave souls walked through our home's red front door for our first service, our small but mighty church plant had described itself as real, relational, and religion-free.

Leading with love and aiming for the radical center theologically—that is, holding the Word and Spirit in tension—as well as politically, we set the tone for being real and relational with each other and God. "Religion-free" was a cheeky way to say we didn't want anything—none of the usual religious trappings, rituals, or expectations—to get in the way of the work God was doing in us and through us as a church.

During every service we gave God time and space, hoping we'd leave church changed by his Spirit. We were real and vulnerable from the stage, sharing our fears, worries, failings, and shortcomings, and we worked to build a church where people felt welcomed and loved and were constantly pointed towards Jesus.

Fourteen years in, as COVID hit, we'd already weathered a lot as a church and a family. But despite that (or maybe because of it), CityChurch was healthy and growing, with people of every age, stage, color, and culture, and even managing to hold in loving tension a relatively wide breadth of theological and political views.

Then, seemingly overnight, fueled by the media, politicians, and even prominent church leaders, our little church became a theological and political tinder box—and everyone in it an expert epidemiologist, theologian, and pyrotechnic. No matter what we did, we were caught in the crossfire.

People we considered friends and an integral part of our church family left without a word because we asked them to wear masks. Others stayed away because they were against meeting in person once the CDC had given the all clear. We couldn't win.

We'd never tried to keep everyone happy and even encouraged people for whom CityChurch wasn't a good fit to find a church where their faith could grow. If that was in sung Eucharist, liturgy, and organ music, we told them to go for it.

But this was different. It felt personal even when it wasn't.

Simultaneously, the wider church seemed to stop loving.

History is littered with the debris of infighting, injustice, and exclusion, all done in the name of Christendom, the Bible, or God himself, and unfortunately the modern-day church often isn't much better. For a group of people charged with loving our neighbors as ourselves and letting our unity point towards God, we, the wider Christian church, have done a pretty poor job.

COVID threw gunpowder onto an increasingly divided church.

While the world looked on, shaking their heads and often their fists, the church began hemorrhaging, its self-inflicted wounds bleeding out on social media.

I just hoped it—and I—could survive.

35

While His People Are Hurting

With a growing list of questions and my faith apparently on the rocks, I began to hear a new depth of anguish in my readers' questions.

Hearing readers' stories and trying to support them is the best bit about being an author. So I love it when my inbox is bursting with emails. Even when those stories break me.

Most of us have questioned God and felt our faith shaken at times. That's normal. But when I asked my readers in an email, "What would you ask God if you got the chance?" the questions poured in, holding a new longing, pain, and lostness I hadn't heard before:

- Why won't you answer me? I need you. Why don't you come?

- Why can't I feel you when I've been begging you just to let me sense you . . . ?

- Why do things happen one on top of each other? What does it take to catch a break?

- Why did you put me in a family that causes so much damage and lifelong pain?

- Were we praying wrong? Did we not ask correctly? Why did you let my son die?

- What happened to my relationship with you?

- Why do I hear great biblical truths at church, but those same church people reject me?

Pain and urgency cried out from my inbox.

If these questions sound familiar, please know you're not alone or the exception, and your faith isn't flawed.

Questions we have about God and for God often spring first from our pain. And if there's one thing I know about pain, it's that it always feels personal. When life is good, we might intellectually wonder, *Why does God allow suffering?* But when we are the ones who are raped or abandoned, or it's our five-year-old with the terminal diagnosis, the pain and questioning become deeply personal and far more desperate.

As we sheltered in place during the worst of the pandemic, the scenes of mortuaries lining the streets of NYC, nurses in hazmat suits, and schools working to help feed (let alone educate) kids competed for media space with forest fires in Australia, the port explosion in Beirut, deadly hurricanes in South America, and locust swarms across Africa and Asia.

Had God fallen asleep at the wheel? Where was he? Why didn't he do something?

When my personal pain joined the collective lament of both my reader community and our wider suffering world, it became one more car careening into the multivehicle pileup of my beaten-up faith, setting God in a new, fragile light.

When our church loses its way, the worldwide church appears to stop loving, and God's people hurt deeply, we look to Scripture for comfort and guidance. We seek out old familiar verses worn smooth with telling and alive with hope. But sometimes our pain is just too much, and it's not hope we find in Scripture but confusing, indifferent harshness.

And the Bible Looks Different

Imagine you're scrolling through your newsfeed and a horrific headline stops you dead.

EVIL MURDERER ESCAPES DEATH PENALTY.
JUDGE SENTENCES MURDERER'S SON INSTEAD.

Then another.

JUDGE REWARDS LEADER WITH THRONE
AFTER LEADER FOUND GUILTY OF TRICKING
AND SLAUGHTERING TEMPLE WORSHIPERS

Then another.

DEATH OF ALL TWO-YEAR-OLDS ORDERED BY KING

We'd be horrified beyond belief. Yet with God's presence, permission, and even command (see 2 Sam. 12:1–23; 2 Kings 9–10; Matt. 2:16–18), we're often encouraged to accept these biblical atrocities without question, adequate context, or true exploration, and to focus solely on God's faithfulness, provision, and promises. With everything else stirring within me, it wasn't that simple.

The stories weren't new, but the sense of injustice they fueled within me was.

Was this slaughter really necessary, God? Wasn't there another way?

And why did you set the people of Israel up to fail from the get-go, demanding they keep impossible laws, knowing you'd ultimately send your Son?

I just don't get it.

The Bible, despite being a symbol of hope and promise for a huge chunk of humanity, has also led to centuries of pain and destruction in the name of religion. I often find it easier to reconcile man's inhumanity to man than God's apparent inhumanity towards us, his children. After all, we—not God—are the broken ones with a propensity towards control, power, and greed.

But these stories can make a girl wonder.

Once again I found myself asking whether the answers I'd always found comfort in still held up.

Or did God simply need a better PR team?

Had I been sold a bait and switch before selling it to others in a gospel-cloaked pyramid scheme? Was I "selling" people a God of love and abundant life only for them to discover he's fickle, his church is woefully lacking in grace for the hurting and marginalized, and our faith in him can be so easily obscured by politics and division?

Were Bible stories simply "a category of superhero comic" and "not to be confused with real life"?[2]

Where Does That Leave Us?

These questions and my readers' stories of devastating pain and loss—despite knees calloused from prayer—collided with my futile attempts to find clarity. My old, buried questions were resurrected by fresh frustrations with the God of the Bible, the church handing out rejection and spiritual abuse, and the political activists dishing out hate and division under Jesus placards and crosses.

Doubt hung threateningly over my constant reassurances to myself and others that God is good, even if life isn't. The questions and confusion demanded attention I was reluctant to give.

When the certainty we once stood on begins to fade, our connection, intimacy, and belonging with God fade too.

> When the certainty we once stood on begins to fade, our connection, intimacy, and belonging with God fade too.

Over time, as my relationship with God dwindled, my most pressing question became not *Can I find certainty again?* but *Can I rediscover the latter without demanding the former?* I prayed I could. But the only thing keeping me from turning away altogether was a kernel of belief hidden within a shell of hope. Like the desperate father of the dying boy in Mark 9:14–29, all I could pray was "Lord, I believe. Help my unbelief."

Suddenly, I was embarrassed to call myself a believer; telling people we led a church became loaded with assumptions about what we stood against rather than for.

I believed in God. I still loved Jesus. I was certain I still wanted him in my life, and I still trusted him, even though articulating why was trickier. It was everything *else* I struggled with.

If I still believed in God, what was I really doubting? His goodness, trustworthiness, or his ways? More importantly, were these doubts deal-breakers? Was this it? Was my faith and my call to encourage people towards God crumbling? How could I write about trusting God when I wasn't sure I liked him, even if I still, ironically, loved him?

Could I, like Rachel Held Evans, conclude that I was still a Christian "because the story of Jesus is still the story I'm willing to risk being wrong about"?[3]

There's a type of grief called ambiguous loss. First used by researcher Pauline Boss in the 1970s, it describes the loss we experience when there is physical presence but psychological absence, such as when dementia leaves a parent unrecognizable and absent in all but their physical presence.[4] Could I be experiencing a type of spiritual ambiguous loss in my relationship with God? I knew he was present, but I didn't recognize him or his people anymore.

Like Job and David, I had big questions that demanded attention. They held urgency. I wanted to act. But I also wanted to bury them. Should I stay or go? Neither option felt viable or sat well with me. But if I ran, I'd have to answer the question

Peter asked when Jesus gave him the chance to turn away like so many others had: "Where else would I go?" (see John 6:68–69).

I knew God was very real—it's just that life with him had become more complicated, and I was running out of energy to fight for our relationship.

With the ever-present temptation to walk away wooing me, I buried my head like an ostrich. There was no soaring on wings like eagles. No running and not growing weary, no walking without fainting, and very little strength being renewed (Isa. 40:31). Keeping my faith was exhausting. Actively pursuing God slid to the bottom of my to-do list.

Despite the doom and gloom, an undeniable flicker of hope and faith somehow remained. And for those of us who've boomeranged from lost to found and back again, this tiny flicker stokes our belief we're not as lost as we fear.

You might not know if you're a believer, a doubter, a believing doubter, or a doubting believer—or something else entirely. Maybe you're not lost, but you're not exactly found anymore either. Perhaps, like me, you're in no-man's-land, oscillating between the two. Wherever you find yourself today, it's okay. It's not just you, you're not the only one, and this doesn't mean you're doing something wrong or your faith's disintegrating.

We might be at the crossroads of faith and doubt, wondering how we got here, but our question must now be, Which way next?

God, let me think about this for a minute . . .

Take a moment to reflect on your story and work out your current spiritual GPS location so you can begin to understand and move forward in your own journey. The following questions will help.

- How does my story resonate with yours?

- In the following lists, check all that apply to you today. Be 100 percent honest, even checking them all if you want to! (You're simply naming where you're at today. There's no similar checklist in the last chapter to "test" how far you've come—this isn't that kind of book!)

  At the moment I'd call myself a . . .
  - ☐ Believer
  - ☐ Doubter
  - ☐ Doubting believer
  - ☐ Believing doubter
  - ☐ Skeptic
  - ☐ Something else (add your own descriptor)
  - ☐ I'm not sure

  At the moment I feel . . .
  - ☐ Disillusioned
  - ☐ Hurt
  - ☐ Worried
  - ☐ Far from God
  - ☐ Frustrated
  - ☐ Embarrassed
  - ☐ Confused
  - ☐ Holding on by a thread
  - ☐ Angry
  - ☐ Something else (add how you feel)

- Think about the last time you were physically lost. How did it feel being lost? How did you find your way to where you needed to be? How did your mood and outlook change when you found your way again?

- Where in your faith do you feel most lost? Check all that apply.

  ☐ Church

  ☐ Personal pain

  ☐ Global unrest and suffering

  ☐ Unanswered prayer

  ☐ Other Christians

  ☐ The Bible

  ☐ Relationship with God

  ☐ Uncertainty

  ☐ Something else (name it here) _____

- What's the biggest thing(s) or experience(s) that has made you feel this way?

- Name your biggest, hairiest, most urgent, God-question that's causing you to doubt him.

When You Get to the Fork in the Road, Ignore It

While I was sitting around the fire with some friends one night, the topic of my next book came up. Though it was still just a seed of an idea, I had an inkling of what I wanted to write about but hadn't nailed down a back-cover-worthy description or interest-piquing pitch. But these were close friends and I trusted the heart behind the question, so I dove in. Throwing out words like *certainty*, *doubt*, *questions*, *intimacy*, and *relationship* like they were party favors, I finally zeroed in on the questions I'd been wrestling with privately.

"I think the book is really about what we do when we get to the crossroads of doubt and faith and whether doubt really is the swear word many of us have been conditioned to believe, or if it can be a force for good God can use." Examining their faces, I looked around, curious to see if these questions resonated.

Tom, a spiritually thoughtful educator who'd been a head teacher for years, paused graciously. "I don't like the term *doubt*. It implies negative bias; minds already moving towards the exit. Semantics matter. I prefer *wonder*."

I smiled. He'd nailed the problem of doubt. He'd articulated the fear behind our fears and the negative bias doubt can't shake. We assume it's negative, inevitably leads to a crumbling faith, and must linger like an unshakable bad smell once we've wrestled within its grip. The thought of admitting we're questioning fills us with dread. So let me encourage you: Doubt isn't the beginning of losing faith. How can I be so sure?

Doubt isn't the beginning of losing faith.

Firstly, research shows that deconstruction (if that's even what we're doing) is not the same as deconversion, nor does it inevitably lead to the end of faith.[5] In other words, not everyone who questions walks away.

Secondly, since you're reading this book, I'm pretty confident you don't want to lose your faith. It's too precious to you. Even if your faith changes over time, you'd rather not lose it altogether.

Thirdly, and most importantly, I truly believe God never lets us go. Not in a creepy, abusive, cultish kind of way, but in an "I love you so much. Your free will is my gift. Go, if that's what you choose, but I'm always here, loving you, wooing you, fighting for you" kind of way.

Your questions, concerns, and frustrations tell me your faith is very much alive, even if it doesn't look or feel as cozy and comforting as you'd like. Doubting might feel like the beginning of the end of your faith, but I believe if we let it, doubt can be *the end of the beginning*. It's time to ignore the fork in the road.

The Great Conversation

My dad had (and still has) the most annoying quips and quotes he'd come out with over dinner, a school report, or in the car. The setting wasn't the point. His goal was to transform whatever my sisters and I were up to into either a groan-worthy moment or, worse, a teachable one. His little sayings drove us bonkers, but most of them have (much to my annoyance) stuck. His favorite, when we were struggling with a big decision, was this little gem:

When you get to the fork in the road, ignore it.

Well thanks, Dad. That clears things up.

It was nonsensical. A fork in the road is impossible to ignore. The whole point is you *have* to choose. Not choosing isn't an option, unless you want to head back the way you came. Or so younger Niki assumed.

My faith had now come to a fork in the road, the way forward splitting in front of me—faith one way, doubt the other. Neither felt right, but equally I couldn't simply retrace my steps. Finally, five decades later, the penny dropped, and Dad's age-old encouragement made sense. Maybe it wasn't the obtuse, unsolvable riddle I'd always assumed, but a call to think outside the box. To never assume the path is set or that there are only two options, but to search for alternatives lying hidden from view.

Sitting at this particular fork in the road, many of us can't see beyond the two paths of faith and doubt. Which one is right? Which one leads back to the comfort of the faith we've known and loved? For so long, everything GodFaithChurch, had led me to dig in and hold my ground, assuming that finding and having answers was paramount—the only way to follow the path of faith.

Opportunities to wrestle with God and the biblical text were more than plentiful. But unlike Jacob, who wrestled God through the night until God blessed him (see Gen. 32), I didn't relish coming away with a limp, which meant I limited how hard and long I'd fight before crying Uncle. It was easier to echo the "winner-take-all" refrain Rachel Held Evans talked about: "The Bible said it; I believe it; that settles it."[6] Until it wasn't.

In contrast, there's something warmer, gentler, and more welcoming about the Jewish midrash interpretation of Scripture, where the tensions and questions it produces "aren't obstacles to be avoided, but rather opportunities for engagement, invitations to join in the Great Conversation between God and God's people that has been going on for centuries and to which everyone is invited."[7] And as I read of this desire on God's part for open, honest conversation about our questions, a chink of light emerged. Could this be another way? Was I so engaged in the Great Commission I'd missed my invitation to the Great Conversation? What would happen if I went directly to God with the stomach-churning, mind-contorting Scriptures and wrestle-worthy issues around GodFaithChurch? If I asked, *What were you thinking, Lord?* would he pull up his celestial sofa, mug of tea in hand, and happily sit down to chat?

This glimmer of light became the welcoming invitation I needed to keep going, so I pressed on. This time less defensively, more openly willing to wrestle and engage with God, even to leave without answers and with, perhaps, a slight holy hobble.

The more I pondered our invitation to this Great Conversation, the more I saw how folks like Moses, Job, Sarah, Elizabeth, and Hagar had ignored the fork in the road when they struggled, and instead entered a wonderful holy dialogue with God. They boldly asked questions, wrestled, and even pushed back on perceived wisdom. Could I—dare I—join them?

Joining the great cloud of witnesses in this Great Conversation keeps our eyes fixed on God. It keeps our hearts, and even our fists, pointed towards him. Talking with God is, after all, the real point of faith: a living, breathing, walking, talking relationship. It's not figuring him out or putting him in a neat, convenient box we can carry with us wherever life takes us.

In his wonderful book *Let Your Life Speak*, author and educator Parker J. Palmer advocates, "Before you tell your life what you intend to do with it, listen for what it intends to do with you."[8] For years I'd told my faith what it *should* look like, but now I began to listen for what it (aka God) wanted to tell me it could be.

For those of us who've answered the call to pull our faith up by its bootstraps or yank up the roots of our doubt with blind faith, only to find ourselves spiritually exhausted and with our faith as cracked and fragile as when we first doubted . . . it's time to throw in the towel. Not on our faith, but on trying to figure it out alone.

It's time to ignore the fork in the road and chat with God.

The Opposite of Doubt Isn't Faith

Opposites are funny fish. When we've had a crazy-hard day, we say our life and house are in complete disarray and we look unkempt and disheveled. Yet, when it's been a brilliant day and we've rocked everything from our outfit to our to-do lists, we don't say our life's in *array* or that we look utterly *kempt* and fabulously *sheveled*.

Is the opposite of doubt faith? Or is it trust, belief, or possibly certainty? What about *undoubt*, as in unbelievable? *Disdoubt*, as in disagree? *Imdoubt*, as in implausible?

I'm kidding, but you get my point. It's not clear what the opposite of doubt is exactly.

Merriam-Webster lists sixteen antonyms for *doubt*. Words like *trust, belief, confidence,* and *certainty*. Then there are the less obvious yet equally compelling words such as *reliance* (on or upon), *certitude, sureness,* and *credence*.[9]

As we go in search of appropriate *doubt* antonyms, many of us find them frustratingly intangible and more slippery than a baby seal on a Slip 'N Slide. Words like *confidence* and *surety* become harder to define and nail down than we'd hoped. How confident is confident enough? Is it possible to be absolutely certain—and more importantly, stay certain?

People who tell me they're utterly, unwaveringly sure of God make me slightly nervous. The skeptic in me wants to question their assurances. *Really? Don't you ever question God? Haven't*

49

you ever *wondered what he's up to or why he does things that seem so wildly out of character—unloving, hurtful, even mean and spiteful? Doesn't a tiny part of you worry it's all just a feel-good party for the disillusioned?*

What we need and our souls long for isn't more of something but more of someone.

Pitching faith against doubt exacerbates the sense that one is right and the other is wrong. It highlights the negative bias my friend Tom was talking about, which only increases our faith-shame and fuels our desire to avoid doubt at all costs. What we need isn't more faith-shame or shoulds or to rummage through our stash of doubt-proof answers for the silver bullet. What we need is gentle encouragement to chat with God, to ask our questions, and to grow our faith and relationship with God. One doubt at a time.

My sense of sureness and trust in God can blow away on a breeze without warning, yet it's stayed when I wouldn't have blinked if it had left without a *thanks, it was good while it lasted*. What we need and our souls long for isn't more of some-*thing* but more of some*one*.

The Opposite of Doubt Begins with Relationship

If you've ever had the joy of having a ride-or-die friend, you know the more time we spend with someone, the more stuff we go through together, the more closely knit we become. The same is true of God. The more we hang out with him, the better we know him and the more we want to keep hanging out.

Matthew, Mark, and Luke all tell the story of a conversation Jesus and his disciples had as they came to the region of Caesarea Philippi, an area known for pagan rituals, worshiping other gods, and even child sacrifice. We can imagine the disciples walking in step with Jesus, the road stretching before them. Over the previous months they'd looked on in awe as Jesus performed miracle after miracle. They'd listened in wonder to his parables about the kingdom of God and had their world turned upside down as he encouraged the weak, grieving, timid, merciful, and persecuted that they were the ones who were blessed. Then, Jesus had divided them into pairs and sent them out with enough spiritual power and authority to heal diseases and deal with any evil opposition they might encounter. Now they were back. Reunited on the dusty roads in the foothills of Caesarea Philippi, Jesus asks them a direct question, apparently without a word of preamble or warning: "Who do the crowds say I am?" (Luke 9:18).

The disciples' answer seems remarkably casual, as if Jesus had asked them who everyone thinks the next James Bond will be. "Some say John the Baptist; others say Elijah; and still others, that one of the prophets of long ago has come back to life" (v. 19).

Jesus's next question must have cut the atmosphere with a knife. Did he pause, letting the dust settle at his feet before continuing? Did he raise an eyebrow at their apparent disinterest? We'll never know, but the big, fat, juicy "BUT" he continues with tells us another answer mattered far more.

"BUT what about you?" he asked. "Who do YOU say I am?" (v. 20, emphasis mine).

In this easy-to-miss three-letter word, Luke seems to imply Jesus wasn't that interested in the crowds' views but was utterly focused on what his closest friends—the guys he'd be leaving in charge of his ministry—thought. What did *they* think?

Jesus didn't ask, "Do you understand what I'm doing?" or "Do you agree with me?" or even "Do you trust me?"

As far as I can tell from reading the Gospels, Jesus never asked his disciples or any of us to agree, be certain, or understand. Instead, he encouraged them—and in turn us—to ask *who* we think he is, to believe *in* him, and to be in relationship *with* him.

For many of us, believing followed understanding. We heard the gospel message, saw our own sinful, yucky side and lack of a way to save ourselves, and understood the equation of Jesus taking our place on the cross. Only then did we say yes to the outrageous grace and mercy of the transaction. We wanted Jesus to take the wheel and steer the train wreck of our lives so we could enjoy the peace, abundant life, and love that came free with our simple yes.

We weren't believers until we were. With a simple yes, we arrived. Our job now was to stay there. To become more like Jesus and, in turn, more certain of what we believe.

Saying yes to Jesus all those years ago and telling him, along with the familiar faces around the water-filled dumpster in our London church, how I knew *who* he was and *what* he'd done for me, felt like coming home. As I dipped below the water, I belonged. This was home. My job was to settle in, become more Christlike, and tell every poor soul I knew how brilliantly amazing he is. (I admit, I was a little over-enthusiastic at times in those early days.)

Maybe if I'd seen belief not as a destination (or even a starting point) but as a natural by-product of my relationship with God, everything would have felt a little easier, less pressured and weighty.

This idea has a rightness about it. It's not just theologically sound (*phew!*) but our stuck selves only have one thing to do: get to know someone better. We don't have to figure everything out or do intellectual gymnastics worthy of an Olympic theologian. We don't even have to set ourselves the goal of certainty. All our poor, stuck, doubt-wrestling selves need to do is find one simple way to get to know God better. Then rinse and repeat.

> All our poor, stuck, doubt-wrestling selves need to do is find one simple way to get to know God better. Then rinse and repeat.

Play an imaginary game with me for a second. Imagine you've got a really close friend you love dearly. You hang out together—a lot. You go on vacations, text constantly, borrow each other's Spanx, and there isn't anything she doesn't know about you. She held you when your dad died and calls you out when you're pigheaded. You trust her, love her, believe in her, and are sure it's mutual.

Then, slowly over time, things start to change.

Your texts and calls go unanswered. Her friend group shifts and they make you uneasy. She's aloof and distant, and on the rare occasions you get together there's an enormous, fidgeting elephant in the room neither of you dares mention.

Wouldn't your belief in your friend—her goodness, trustworthiness, and love—begin to crumble? Mine would. Maybe I'd hurt her or unknowingly annoyed her, or perhaps someone had bad-mouthed me and she'd believed them. Eventually, I'd wonder if she and everything I trusted had all been a sham.

Hopefully that hasn't happened to you, but since you're reading this book, the chances are it feels like this with God.

If we had an issue like this with a friend, we'd get the same advice from our mums, therapists, and social media gurus:

"Go and talk to her!"
"Hear her side of the story."
"Tell her how hurt you are."
"Listen to how she feels about you."
"Forgive her."
"Your friendship is worth it."

There's no guarantee we'd get satisfactory answers, but slowly we'd begin to rebuild our relationship. Inch by inch we'd get to know each other again as we show up, listen, and are honest and heartfelt.

You might never find certainty, but you'll rekindle intimacy and belief in one another.

And wasn't that what we loved in the first place?

Intimacy fuels belief. Belief fuels intimacy.

Distraught, Defiant, and Daring

Job was quite a guy—an honest man, devoted to God, wealthy beyond belief, and one of the most influential men in all the East. With a big family, cattle, land, good friends, and influence, he'd enjoyed a pretty sweet life until God and Satan played chicken with his faith. The goal was simple: test Job's faithfulness to see if it was genuine, simply a bonus of enjoying the good life, or even a way to keep God happy and ensure health and prosperity. The stakes were high, the players defiant, leaving Job and his family unprotected in sniper's alley (see Job 1).

An unbelievable string of disasters follows. Job's livestock, servants, and children are killed in a single day before Job himself is covered in painful sores. Yet still Job worships God. He even defends God to his wife and friends, who assume Job's done something to deserve this suffering. In their understanding, things go wrong when you do something wrong.

Yet, as Eugene Peterson notes in his introduction to the book of Job in *The Message*, "Job was doing everything right when suddenly everything went wrong."[10]

Most of us understand that hard things happen. What throws us into doubt and confusion is undeserved suffering. The baby who dies in its mother's arms just moments after taking its first breath. The teenager drowning in anxiety and hidden depression who believes the world, and especially his family, would be better off without him. The woman beaten physically and emotionally by a jealous partner for smiling at the checkout boy.

The injustice of our pain is palpable when we've tried our hardest to do everything right—to be the best woman, sister, friend, employee, neighbor, mother, believer, worshiper, small group leader, volunteer, and human we can be.

We're left reeling, outraged, incredulous, doubting, questioning, and tempted to walk away. And it's understandable.

My cancer, so soon after losing Mum and Jo, left me asking the same questions Job asked of God. *Why? Why me? Justify yourself!*

Outrageously for his time, Job takes his questions straight to God—not to teachers, philosophers, doctors, or gurus. "He refused to take silence for an answer. He refused to take clichés for an answer. He refused to let God off the hook."[11]

It's easy to hear Job's side of the conversation with our New Testament ears, which are familiar with the idea of God speaking to regular folks through his Spirit. But in Job's time, the Holy Spirit spoke to certain people at certain times to accomplish certain things. Access to God and answers from God came through priests, sacrifices, the temple, or prophets, not the daily conversation Jesus has enabled it to be. In his pain, exhaustion, and confusion, Job cut out the middleman and went straight to God, refusing to take answers from anyone else. He was unrelenting, articulate, and passionate. Daring and defiant.

When we dare to question God, he doesn't admonish us for being impertinent but invites us to hang out together in the mystery.

On the one hand, God's answer is deeply annoying and unsatisfying: *You're not me and could never understand the complexity, enormity, and mystery of all I hold in the palm of my hand.* We want answers, not riddles or unsolvable puzzles. On the other hand, it's equally, if not more so, a relief. When we dare to question God, he doesn't admonish us for being impertinent but invites us to hang out together in the mystery.

Worried my faith was slipping away, disheartened by the state of the church, and turned off God by the hurtful actions of those who say they love him, I followed Job's lead and persistently and passionately went to God with my questions. Not bold enough to think God might whisk me off on a cosmic, visionary journey, I was pretty sure he'd show up in other ways, the ways he makes himself known to us all—from majestic sunsets and the grandeur of the heavens to the warmth of a friend's hug or an unexpected peace in the midst of our panic.

What we see in Job isn't a man who hung on to his faith because he had his intellectual and spiritual need for certainty placated. Far from it. What we find is a broken man asking very human questions. A man humbled by the majesty and complexity of God yet utterly confident of who he is to him. A man willing to walk out the mystery of faith in conversation with God.

If we constantly try to wrestle our doubts into intellectual submission, we have to ask ourselves where this rodeo wrangling is taking us. In circles? Away from God? To bed? Out the side door unnoticed? Digging in? A bit of everything? Wherever it's going, it's exhausting. Aren't you tired? I am.

Jesus offers an invitation to the poor, weary, and heavy laden like us: "Come to me, . . . and I will give you rest" (Matt. 11:28). It's the same invitation at the heart of Job's story: to come to God with it all, to be willing to hold all our concerns and questions in tension with the unboxable, unfathomable mystery of God and simply rest in him. If we graciously accept, we might never find certainty, but we will discover the kind of relationship with God we've been searching for all along.

So I told God, "I don't get it."

He seemed to answer with a smile that tickled his eyes: *That's okay. You're not meant to. The only thing I want you to "get" is my love. The rest is frosting.*

Eventually, over time and with his help, this other way of walking with him through life and faith's mystery became clearer, more natural, and even more comfortable. I learned to talk with him about it all, bringing everything—from my wondrous awe at his creation to the ugly underbelly of my wrestlings and even the unknowns and longings I didn't have words for. I'd walk and talk to the sky, the trees, the wind, even the dog, confident God was listening. My journal filled with lines of frantic scrawl as I listened to what he might be saying. It wasn't easy. I've heard it said God never speaks with such certainty that there's no room for doubt, and I'm sure anyone who's tried to discern his voice can relate. But he does give us a sense, a nudge, or a whisper, and we're better off listening than not.

Sitting in mystery became my new ground zero, my norm. As a scientist at heart, I've always wanted answers and proof and looked for assurances I was on the right track. But that's not what God gave Job, so, unsurprisingly, I never found it either. But the scientist in me also knew I'd regret the questions I didn't ask more than the ones I did. And so, despite the unease of uncertain mystery, I began to lean into the uncomfortable questions, even get used to them. For black-and-white-thinking Niki, it might have felt like sitting on a bed of nails, but for disillusioned-yet-curious Niki, it was a welcome relief as slowly the heaviness began to lift.

Reignite, Reimagine, or Re(Whatever You Need)

With our faith panties all wadded up, it's easy to miss Jesus's invitation to come to him and find rest for our souls (Matt. 11:28). When we and the churches we visit spend more time and energy figuring God out and teaching *about* him than meeting or talking *with* him, it's no wonder we're left lost and wondering whether our Shepherd is on vacation, has given up, or wasn't as caring as his résumé suggested.

With the central tenets of our faith being inherently relational—"the Word made flesh," Jesus's death and resurrection uniting us with God, and the Holy Spirit as counselor and guide—it's a shame we either miss God's simple invitation to intimacy and rest, or we don't know how to take Jesus up on his offer. Or perhaps something else is holding us back.

Women like Julian of Norwich, who witnessed the devastating suffering of the Black Death, the schism of the Catholic church, and the horrific consequences of a long, drawn-out war, were still able to say, "All shall be well, and all shall be well, and all manner of thing shall be well."[12] Not because they had the answers, but because they lived in continual conversation with God.

It's as if they heard God whisper, *Come to me. This crossroads isn't a place of shame, fear, and sadness, forcing you to pick one path over another. It's a place of acceptance, curiosity, conversation, and intimacy with me. Why not unpack, stay awhile, and talk?*

We don't stop praying because we lose faith. We lose faith because we stop talking to God.

We don't stop praying because we lose faith. We lose faith because we stop talking to God.

Our invitation from Jesus is simple: come to him, follow him, and learn from him. That's it. No wonder his burden is light. There are no hoops to jump through, boxes to check, or rules to follow. Nothing heavy to lug around. With a very different view of the Scriptures than the religious leaders of his day, Jesus's gospel was and is one of outrageous grace. He doesn't say his burden is light and his way is easy because it's flimsy or wishy-washy but because he's the one who does the heavy lifting. Our job is simply to respond, follow along, and learn from him as best we can.

I wish I could guarantee that your faith will transform the moment you embrace this new way of thinking and sit in the mystery in conversation with God, or that embracing doubt will feel so natural you'll wonder why you never did it before. But spiritual transformation and the work of shifting our mind-set takes time. So does learning to chat with God in this new way. As much as we'd like to, we can't rush ahead. Instead, as Pierre Teilhard de Chardin encourages, we must "trust in the slow work of God."[13] For that is what it is—his work, not ours.

Slowness and inactivity isn't my jam—just ask my kids how fast I walk—so I know how excruciatingly passive trust can feel. We want change and we want it now! Thankfully, we have a part to play, because learning to sit in mystery and talk with God doesn't just happen while we sit back and twiddle our thumbs, impatient for God to do his thing. Doubt is a verb—a *doing* word, as my elementary school teacher, Mrs. Knox, would have said. Doubt is active. It invites motion, conversation, debate, and listening. It's holy, intimate work.

Especially when we engage in conversation with the one we're doubting. If, as it's been said, holy envy is seeing God at work in the faith traditions of others,[14] could holy doubt be the gift of seeing God at work in the wrestlings of our faith?

Even if we don't realize it, most of us have a few wonky beliefs about God, doubts, and what might happen if we dare to doubt that prevent us from showing up wide open and honest. So before sitting down to chat with him, we need to deal with them and set ourselves free.

God, let me think about this for a minute . . .

Would you like to RSVP "yes" to Jesus's invitation to rest, conversation, and holy doubt? If so, let's disarm those doubts by getting rid of some of the rubbish we believe about our faith and doubts. Take a moment and do these guided exercises as honestly as you can.

- Grab two paper plates (dinner plates will do if you don't have paper), on one write MY FAITH. On the other, MY DOUBTS (obviously, don't write on your bone china! Just write on sticky notes and stick them to your plates). Place your faith and doubt plates as close together or as far away from each other as you imagine your faith and doubt to be in real life. Let them overlap as much or as little as you think they do. Perhaps they're separate on either side of the room, maybe they're overlapping just slightly, or they might be so together there's only a sliver of one or the other poking out. You decide. You're creating a kind of Venn diagram.

- Does where you've placed your plates—how far apart or close together they are—surprise you? If so, why? Did you know immediately where to place them or did you have to think about it and move them a few times?

- As you look at your circles, imagine Jesus giving them a nudge in one direction or another as a gentle invitation to be more honest with yourself and him. How does he move them? How do you react?

- Reassure yourself of Jesus's love and that he's not judging your faith or doubt, then take a moment to sit with him in the space between your plates or where they overlap and just be together. No need to talk. Simply enjoy his loving presence. When you're ready, respond to his invitation in your own words.

PART 2

God, Is This True?

From Myth to Mantra

Faith and doubt go hand in hand,
they are complementaries.
One who never doubts will never truly believe.

—Herman Hesse

Unlearning Our Doubt Myths

Whether it's *Romeo and Juliet*, *Pride and Prejudice*, or *Pretty Woman*, romances follow a familiar and well-loved path. Boy and girl meet—or boy and dragon rider meet, depending on your genre—boy and girl overcome some kind of conflict, undying love is confessed, and they live happily ever after. Who doesn't love the familiarity and predictability of a good romance?

For the soon-to-be star-crossed lovers, the conflict normally revolves around a popcorn tub's worth of misplaced assumptions about one another, driving them apart rather than into each other's arms. Whether she thinks he's arrogant when really he's shy (Mr. Darcy of *Pride and Prejudice*), or he assumes his job stands in their way (Hugh Grant's Prime Minister in *Love Actually*), the result is the same—the distance and tension (romantic or otherwise) grow. Finally, moments before the credits roll, in a heartwarming or hilarious moment, clarity dawns. The lovers' rift vanishes. The scales fall from their eyes and finally they see each other's true self. Once again (as if we ever doubted) love wins, and we mop up the tears of a happy ending.

Sadly (or is it thankfully?) real life isn't a Hallmark movie. Don't get me wrong. I love a happy ending as much as the next person, but wouldn't it be a relief if our assumptions and misunderstandings about each other and God didn't get a chance to do their destructive work and drive a wedge between us? Because when they do, our relationships suffer and our happy endings fail to materialize. When I've had a rubbish day and all I want to do is download to Al the moment he walks through the door, but he seems distant and uninterested, I retreat to the bathtub to brood, assuming he doesn't care. Yet the truth is often less sinister—he's had a rough day too, is running on fumes, and just needs a moment to regroup. But by the time I'm immersed in bubbles, the damage has been done.

We might not call them lies (it sounds a bit harsh), but the unquestioned assumptions we live by hold power. Inside these unchallenged perceptions are the deep, cancerous threads of what kind of person we are (too much, not enough, a failure, disorganized, shy), who God is (harsh, fickle, uncaring), and how he feels about us (disappointed, ashamed, mad, or ambivalent). There are even ingrained lies about the doubts themselves (they're destructive, unholy, or unchristian) and whether it's wise to admit them to God (nope, not a good idea) or anyone else (no again). No matter the lie or where it comes from, it holds relationship-crippling potential. If lies excel at anything, it's creating fear and wrecking communication.

Unnamed and unquestioned lies may remain silent, but they're never powerless.

Daring to doubt has given me the chance to reevaluate my long-held assumptions about doubting. Not because my relationship with God is suddenly bomb-proof and I've gained Solomon-worthy levels of holy wisdom. Quite the opposite. Becoming increasingly lost and distant from God, while coming to the end of myself and nearly chucking it all in, afforded me a frightening glimpse of the end of my faith. Only then was I scared enough to ask myself, *What's really holding me back?*

Unnamed and unquestioned lies may remain silent, but they're never powerless. Driving us forward, they determine how we think, feel, and respond to the world and to God. These myths persuade us that talking to God about all we carry is a Very. Bad. Idea. When actually, it's the best thing we can do. Which is why many wiser people than me, like Emily P. Freeman, encourage us to pay attention to what is happening in the unseen places of our souls and name the unnamed.[1]

Only when we've named the unnamed can we question the unquestioned and reclaim the power the lies have wielded unhindered. Then and only then do the whispers of deceit ushering us away from God, daring us to go it alone, fall quiet. So let's ask . . .

Are our unquestioned assumptions about doubt true or just a load of hogwash?

LIE #1: I Need Proof and Answers to Be Sure

Each week during the winter of my senior year in college, I took blood from a hundred Japanese quail. One of my graduation requirements as a zoology major was to assist a PhD student's research and write up our preliminary findings. I was assigned to work with a bespectacled, earnest, socially awkward young chap named John as he studied the biological and physiological changes prior to avian migration. Every Monday I'd climb the spiral stone steps to the old Victorian aviary turret. Then, under the glow of the artificial light and against the pungent smell of freshly encrusted guano, I drew blood and measured the feather growth and molt patterns of a hundred feathered friends.

If you're wondering how you take blood from a bird no bigger than a sparrow, the answer is *carefully*. Nestling the poor little thing on its back in the palm of my left hand, I used that hand's last two fingers to splay out its wing and expose any new feather growth or molt patterns and the tiny vein running across its "elbow." With a tiny needle, I would prick the blood vessel before collecting the blood in an equally small capillary tube. Miraculously, I only had one mishap. Startled by the needle, a young bird flapped its delicate wing before I had a chance to let it go. The sound of its fragile bone snapping, mixed with the stifling heat, the acrid smell, and the thought of what I'd done to this defenseless chap, sent the room spinning. Taking a few calming breaths, I gently closed his wing, returned him to his perch, and headed for the steps to get some fresh air and sunshine.

Apparently, I'd done the right thing, and John reassured me the wing would heal faster than I expected. Sure enough, as I carefully did my rounds the following week, I checked on my little feathered friend and was delighted to see him already starting to heal, the bone setting stronger than before.

In science we're trained from our earliest days to look for answers, proof, and detailed explanation—whether we're in elementary school making ice cream with Ziploc bags of sweetened milk surrounded by ice and salt or doing more rigorous experiments of distillation and titration in high school chemistry. Look hard enough, study and experiment long enough, and we're assured our questions will find answers.

For those of us who grew up in churches where apologetics was an important part of our spiritual formation, we carry the same scientific thinking into our faith. We've grown to believe we *must* have answers if our faith is to stay aloft. Where there are questions, we believe the Bible, theology, and exegesis provide answers. Until they don't. Or not satisfactorily, anyway. Without answers, we're left floundering, our faith wings too fragile to bear our weight. Surely belief and faith without answers is as foolhardy as leaping from a skyscraper and expecting to fly?

That's the lie we've picked up along the way, isn't it? *I need proof and answers to be sure.*

Deep in concerns and questions, feeling lost and disheartened, I felt like a floundering scientist no longer able to prove her life's work but still utterly convinced of its value. Startled by the sharp needles of life, I'd flapped my faith wings and they'd snapped. "Life is hard but God is good," I'd reassure myself, having seen proof in my own life as well as the lives of others. But this was bigger than God's goodness—more confusing, multifaceted, and seemingly unsolvable. Like Thomas, who refused to believe Jesus was alive without the tangible, irrefutable proof of seeing him face-to-face and sticking his fingers into the fresh nail wounds in his hands, I needed answers. Surely answers would gently fold my faith wings back into place, giving them time to mend.

One morning as I sat in front of the fire, tea mug in hand, listening to the Verse of the Day Story from the Bible App, I heard Evan Barber of Axis Media share how, for young people who've grown up in a world of search, information isn't just the end point of searching; it's the key to making *everything* better.[2] He was quoting American sociologist Sherry Turkle's book *Reclaiming Conversation*, and I wanted to write to Sherry and admit it's not just the youngsters who feel this way. Grabbing our phones whenever there's a question about anything— trying to recall the name of the actress in the film we just saw, find somewhere new to go for dinner, or answer our questions about God—has become second nature for my generation as well. Despite growing up watching remoteless TVs, talking on phones attached to the wall, and thinking that making a mixtape was the epitome of high-tech "cool," like Gen Z, we default to finding answers, believing information has the power to make everything, including our relationship with God, better.

That's Ridiculous!

A Daringly Honest Story of Doubt Based on John 20

"Oh good grief, Thomas. What more do you need?"

Peter looked at me with those eyes. Piercing, loving, yet challenging. He was convinced he'd seen Jesus in the flesh, even spoken to him. Said his tomb was empty. Apparently, Jesus had then shown up when Peter and the rest of the guys were together, but I wasn't so sure.

I wanted proof—tangible evidence I could touch and feel.

The last three years had been unbelievable. We followed Jesus from the Mount of Olives to Mount Hermon, and I knew I'd follow him to the ends of the earth. It was the way he utterly loved us and everyone he met. How he saw into our deepest places and loved us deeper, no matter what ugliness, shame, or depravity he found there.

But don't get me wrong. He wasn't a pushover, all meek and mild. Just ask the money changers in the temple or the Pharisees, they'll tell you. They came face-to-face with an entirely different side of the guy. Angry, violent even. He was outraged by what he saw in what he called "his people" and "his Father's house." But there was something else there too. What many didn't see the way we did was the grief. How these things broke his heart.

From what I could tell and all he'd led us to believe, Jesus came to disrupt the world as well as to love it. He was here to save it, and boy do we need saving.

Until he was the one who needed saving.

Arrested, flogged, and brought before Pilate. Yet still he refused to defend himself.

Why? Why didn't you explain yourself, Jesus?

And now he's dead.

From glory and triumph to shameful execution. No wonder we've been hidden away in this stifling, cramped upper room, terrified for our lives and confused. We've no clue what to do, where to go, or who's in charge.

And now Peter's blabbing about the empty tomb. How Jesus showed up *in this room*, standing right where I am now, giving them his peace and even breathing on them.

Sure, Jesus did some pretty weird things; he even mixed his own spit with dirt and wiped it on someone's eyes. But breathing on people? That's just strange. Showing up when you're dead? That's ridiculous.

So what am I meant to think?

That he's alive and well and walking around Jerusalem like it's a normal Monday afternoon? I don't think so. I'm no fool.

If I'm to be convinced, I need to poke my finger into the blood-stained holes left by those crucifixion nails.

I'm no sucker.

Like Thomas, I wanted to know for sure. Investigating the evidence for the resurrection to double-check Jesus was who he said he was is, after all, how I came to faith. However, what we lose in our quest for certainty is curiosity, and the author and scientist in me know how damaging that loss can be.

The lie telling us we need answers and proof steers us away from God and the intimacy we crave, while a curious faith turns us back towards the one we long to know better. If we're not careful, we can swing from believing everything to doubting everything. As Henri Poincaré put it, "To doubt everything or to believe everything [are] two equally convenient solutions; both dispense with the necessity of reflection."[3] Yet, I wonder if what the lie saves us from isn't the work of thinking but the harder work of chatting with God and living in mystery.

Thomas got his proof. Jesus showed up and invited him to step closer, reach out, and poke around in his questions to find his answers. And while we might not get the luxury of seeing Jesus face-to-face in his resurrected body or of feeling the warmth of his breath as he offers us his hands for the proof we're sure we need, Jesus calls us blessed for believing without seeing. Graciously, he puts no demands on our belief, no small print specifying how strong it needs to be or how many answers we must have. Believe with the strength of an ox? You're blessed. Struggling to muster an ounce of subatomic faith dwarfed by even a mustard seed? No worries, you're blessed too.

> **What we lose in our quest for certainty is curiosity.**

Those of us like Thomas, who need to see to believe, who want proof and to know for sure, do ourselves a great disservice if we're not willing to stop telling God what we need and start asking him what he has for us. When we demand answers to our questions, we hold our faith hostage until God pays our ransom and shares his reasons and ways with us. With a knife to the throat of our faith, we're in danger of demanding omniscience as the price of belief.

For God, the endpoint of searching—either him searching for us or us searching for him—isn't information but relationship and intimacy. As we search for God, he in turn searches for us.

As doubting believers and believing doubters, as the blind who see and the seeing who are blind, can we let go of the myth that we need answers and proof to be sure? Can we choose curiosity over certainty, surrendering to uncertainty? Can we embrace the unprovable mystery of God, where Jesus invites those who are questioning to come to him, even calling us blessed for believing, however tentatively or begrudgingly, amidst our doubts?

Killing the Lies

The Myth: I need proof and answers to be sure.

The Mantra: In my doubts, Jesus calls me blessed.

The Reminder: Just as Jesus invited Thomas to poke around in his blood-stained wounds, unfazed by his disciple's doubts, he does the same for us, calling us blessed for believing despite our doubts and without the same in-person opportunity. Taking our doubts to Jesus leads to God's blessing, not the silence or anger we fear.

The Reset: This is your time and space to chat with God about it all. Here are a few questions, prompts, and activities to help you give it a go.

Let's play a game. Grab three cups or glasses and place two upside down and one right side up. Like this.

Your mission, should you choose to accept it, is to turn all three cups right side up in no more than six moves, turning over exactly two cups with each move.

Easy, right?

Now place them with two facing up and one upside down, like this, and try again.

Not so easy, is it?

The reason it's not easy isn't because it takes more than six moves. It's not because you're not good at logic-based problems or didn't go to college. And it's definitely not because you don't have enough faith in yourself.

The truth is, this puzzle isn't just hard—it's unsolvable. No matter how long you work at it, it's impossible to turn all three cups the right way up if you stick to the rules and move two cups at a time.[4]

Thinking about how you felt working on both versions of the puzzle, let me ask you:

- How good did you feel when you solved the easy, first version? Happy? Proud? Intelligent? Skeptical that it was a trick and shouldn't be that simple? Keen to move on to the harder version? In control? Something else?

- What did you think or feel as you tried to solve the unsolvable configuration of cups? Frustrated? Inadequate? Confused? Increasingly angry—with the puzzle or yourself? Like you weren't good/intelligent enough? Did you give up quickly or did you battle on past your allotted six moves?

- How might your reactions to the puzzle mirror your outlook on your faith? Do you feel safe, happy, and calmer when your faith feels solvable? As you've wrestled with the unprovability and unsolvable nature of GodFaithChurch, have you felt similar things to how you felt as you realized the puzzle is unsolvable? (If it makes you feel better, I know I have.)

- How might you make peace with the hard questions you have about God and for God that feel unanswerable and unsolvable?

LIE #2: I'm the Only One

Before we'd agreed to church plant across the pond, let alone labeled our luggage, I'd been warned: "They'll put you on a pedestal. Maybe even call you First Lady." To which I'd snorted in a very unladylike, let alone First Lady–like, manner. *Us? On a pedestal?* It was laughable how not-us that was, but they were right—leading a church seemed to elevate us spiritually in many people's minds. From the moment we landed, we did all we could to publicly leap off that pedestal, sharing our hard stories and questions while welcoming people into our messy, far-from-perfect family life. By showing people we deal with all the same stuff they do, we hoped they'd feel less alone and more able to come to God or us to talk.

The hardest thing about doubt isn't worrying our precious faith is slowly fading or feeling distant from God. It's feeling alone. It's assuming we're the only one thinking these things, the only one whose doubts are quite this bad or who is tempted to walk away.

As Rachel Held Evans admits, "There's nothing quite like going through the motions of Christian life—attending church, leading Bible study, singing hymns, bringing your famous lemon bars to potlucks—while internally questioning the very beliefs that hold the entire culture together. . . . Say something and you risk losing friendships and becoming the subject of gossip. Keep your doubts to yourself and you risk faking it for the rest of your life."[5]

For every hand raised in worship, there's another itching to rise with questions. For every head bowed in prayer, there are others bowed in despondency. Often they're one and the same.

If you've never been part of a community fostering curious faith or discipleship through wrestling, you might well assume no one else questions like you do (or not as deeply, anyway) and everyone's faith is as strong, tough, and deep as it appears on the outside.

We love a good Jacob-worthy wrestling story, but more often than not, the telling is reserved for the post-wrestle lesson. The sun rises on our satiated doubts. We're bestowed the blessing in a red-ribboned box labeled "Unfailing Faith." Our relationship with God is made new. We limp but are stronger for it (and secretly enjoy the "faithful" status it bestows). Everyone loves a happy ending. Messy middles? Not so much.

Red-ribboned stories might foster hope in our God who never leaves, but when we're still mid-wrestle with no end in sight, they can leave us feeling more alone, left behind, or judged than inspired.

Believing we're the only one comes with enough shame and guilt to silence a Taylor Swift concert, so we try our go-to fix— faking it. Promising ourselves it's just for a while, until we get our spiritual mojo back. We go through the motions, ignoring the gnawing chatter of our reservations and the widening gap between us and God.

Faking it works for a while. Worshiping when we least feel like it draws us into God's presence and out of our funk. Giving thanks when we can't see much to be grateful for is proven to lift our spirits and lower stress. Faking it isn't a terrible short-term strategy, but it isn't a stable or life-giving long-term relational strategy. We can't fool ourselves forever. And we can't ever fool

God. Faking it by showing up anyway in an act of obedience to grow our faith is one thing. Faking it to keep up appearances and fool ourselves into believing is another. It doesn't serve us, God, or others.

In truth, we're less alone than we think, and *I'm the only one* is simply an unquestioned assumption with the power to cripple our relationship with God.

Take a stroll with me down the Hebrews 11 Hall of Faith to look at these heroes. This chapter is our happy ending. With its glossy, faith-inspiring bow tying up every vignette, it's easy to forget each story's messy middle. So let's look again.

Hebrews Hall of Faith *and* Doubt

Daringly Honest Stories of Doubt Based on Hebrews 11:4–38 (quoted verses in italics)

By faith Abraham, when called to go to a place he would later receive as his inheritance, obeyed and went, even though he did not know where he was going. By faith he packed up his family and house, yet in doubt passed his wife off as his sister to save his neck. By faith he believed God would fulfill his promises, but when it looked like God wasn't coming through, he questioned his ways and timings and took matters into his own hands by sleeping with his wife's servant to get the promise rolling.

And by faith even Sarah, who was past childbearing age, was enabled to bear children because she considered him faithful who had made the promise. By faith she believed, but not before she'd laughed at the idea and made her husband sleep with her servant because God was taking way too long.

By faith Jacob, when he was dying, blessed each of Joseph's sons, and worshiped as he leaned on the top of his staff. Yet having doubted God as a young man, he continued to struggle with questions into old age, even wrestling with God through the night for a blessing that was already his.

By faith Moses, when he had grown up, refused to be known as the son of Pharaoh's daughter. . . . By faith he left Egypt, not fearing the king's anger, yet he questioned God's choice of him as Israel's leader, asking, "Why me? What do I tell Pharaoh? The people won't trust me or listen to me." *He persevered because he saw him who is invisible.*

I do not have time to tell about Gideon, who doubted God's word so deeply he made him prove it three times, *Barak*, who refused to go into battle unless Deborah led the way, *Samson*, who kept going his own way over God's, and *Jephthah*, who railed at God's unfairness after it was his own rash vow to God that led to his daughter's death. *About David*, who wrote so many songs and poems filled with doubt and questions they've got an entire book of the Bible all to themselves, *and Samuel and the prophets, who through faith conquered kingdoms, administered justice, and gained what was promised, who shut the mouths of lions* but were still very, very human and must have endured moments of disillusionment and crippling doubt.

By faith the disciple Simon became the rock on which the church was built. By faith he preached the gospel and healed the sick, even though he once, in cowardly fear, vehemently denied knowing Jesus, abandoning him to his fate.

By faith Paul became the greatest evangelist and church planter ever known, bringing hundreds to faith through miracles and preaching, even equipping new churches from prison. By faith he endured beatings, shipwrecks, and imprisonment. Yet even he questioned God, begging him to take away the "thorn" in his flesh God was refusing to heal.

In our minds, these original faith influencers live in the spiritual stratosphere. We persuade ourselves they're different. That we're the only ones who struggle and wrestle. Meanwhile, the lie grins on, victorious, gleefully standing between us and an honest chat with God.

Over dinner one night, I dared tell a friend how my doubts and questions were crippling me and my faith and how lost I felt. Quietly, she confided she felt the same. The more I asked around (tentatively at first, nervous of admitting where I was at), the more I came to see how crowded the crossroads of doubt and faith are. As I shared my wrestling, always landing back on the phrase "I once was found but now I'm lost," I saw how less alone I was than I'd assumed. Some friends had just arrived, others had been there awhile, and no one knew what to do or where to go. But everyone was relieved to know they weren't alone.

> In our doubts we might not have answers, but we do have company.

These conversations gave me hope. The relief was enormous. The way forward, even if hidden, was well-worn, and I knew together we'd find it. On top of that, if all these people were wrestling and questioning, I could bet my last piece of communion bread that God already knew and was ready for me. For *us*. In our doubts we might not have answers, but we do have company.

The lie *I'm the only one* has been slain. It's lying lifeless on the floor, and we're free to step over it on our way to coffee with God.

Killing the Lies

The Myth: I'm the only one.

The Mantra: I'm not alone. I'm in great company.

The Reminder: The crossroads of faith and doubt is more crowded than we think. You're on a well-trodden path—not one destined to end with your faith in tatters but in the Hall of Faith alongside the heroes you've long admired.

The Reset: This is your time and space to chat with God about it all—the myth, the mantra, and the reminder. Here are a few questions, prompts, and activities to help you give it a go.

- Make a personal "Hall of Faith and Doubt" list that includes all the people you can think of—friends, family, people at church, pastors, celebrities, authors, and people in the Bible—who've struggled with their faith in some way. Give yourself ten minutes to brainstorm, then keep a running list in a journal or your phone's Notes app. Add to it every time you have a conversation with someone who's feeling the same way as you. Make sure to include yourself!

- Write a short "Dear Future Me" note to remind future you how unalone she is. Be generous with your words of hope and encouragement, inspiring her to keep chatting with God and not walk away. Either write it in on your favorite stationery and pop it in your Bible for whenever you next feel alone, or mail it to me! I'll prayerfully pop it back in the post to you, trusting it will arrive when you need it most. (You can find my mailing address and more instructions at GodCanWeChat.com.)

- Do you know someone who has similar faith struggles? Take a moment to text them an encouraging note in solidarity, giving them hope and reminding them they're not alone and their faith isn't crumbling. Here's one you can use if you like:

  > Hi [first name], I know we've both been struggling with questions in our faith, so I thought I'd remind us both they're not the beginning of the end of our

faith. God's got us and he's not going anywhere. I often forget I'm not the only one who has doubts about things and wanted to let you know you're not alone. Let's chat with God about it!

- Whether you're in your kitchen, on a walk with the dog, or in the shower, shout out loud, "I'm not the only one! I'm in great company! Woo-hoo!" Snap a photo and post it on Instagram (unless you really are in the shower 😉), tagging me @niki.hardy so I can cheer you on.

LIE #3: I Can't Question God

The vast expanse of tan and beige earth stretched out below like a Pinterest board of organic modern, neutral rug recommendations. At thirty-five thousand feet, we cut through a mile and a half of frigid, cloudless troposphere every second, yet still the carpet stretched on. And on. We crossed deserts, national parks, and preserves, with only a sprinkling of towns and oases of green to break up the monochromatic landscape.

Coming from an island that can fit into the US forty times over, the expanse of this country isn't lost on me. America is big—really big. Of course, we know this, but when a vast fissure opened in the earth's crust below us, like something out of a Hollywood earthquake disaster movie, and wove through the arid rock for mile upon mile, I didn't just feel small. I felt microscopic. A dust mote caught in the canyon's thermals. Staring down, I lost myself in the kind of thoughts moments like these provoke: *Who am I to this vast world? What can I add? What am I doing here? I'm just a moment in the ever-turning wonder of time on this planet, and the God who made all this and more made me. Wow.*

Big philosophical questions don't consume me that often (I'm really not that deep!), but when I'm face-to-face with such awe and wonder, they take me down an Alice-sized rabbit hole. From there, it's only a hop and a skip to *Who am I to challenge God or bother him with my "little" questions and hurts?*

Whether we're feeling small and inadequate in a tin can suspended above the Grand Canyon or reading stories of God's mighty smite button annihilating complete cities, it's no wonder we end up believing the lie that says we can't, shouldn't, or it would be extremely unwise to question God. He's God, after all, while we most definitely are not.

Maybe you're hesitant to question God, not because you feel small or nervous in his presence but because you've been warned of his wrath and impatience for anyone who doesn't toe the line or who dares approach his throne with anything less than reverence, repentance, and unquestioning worship.

When my sister Jo was lying in her hospice bed, an oxygen mask easing her last breaths, we held her hand and prayed. At just forty-three, she was dying. The cancer, victorious. She'd survived almost fourteen months, four more than expected, and for that and so much else we were grateful. For everything else, I was angry. Gratitude and anger, not obvious roommates, managed to live together quite happily—until they couldn't. In the days following Jo's death and my own diagnosis weeks later, anger and questions chipped away at my soul and my relationship with God faster than gratitude could rebuild it.

If his plans are always good, what the heck was this? This was not good. It was very, very bad. What was he thinking? Or maybe he wasn't. Maybe he'd forgotten us. But who was I to question God? Surely, questioning his goodness would be a huge black mark on my faith. A whopping D+ on this test I was so obviously failing. Surely as soon as God noticed, he'd shake his head in resigned displeasure. *Oh you of little faith (Matt. 8:26), why didn't you believe and not doubt at all (James*

1:6)? All you had to find was a tiny bit of faith, no bigger than a mustard seed, but you blew it.

So I backed away.

Doubting was one thing. Questioning God directly, in all his might and majesty, wrath and judgment, not to mention holiness, seemed to raise the stakes. Foolish at best, dangerous if taken too far, risking rejection. The lie won, remaining unnamed, unquestioned, and as powerful as ever.

Mr. Owen was my elementary school head teacher, and he called me "Knickers." It was the '70s. Nicknames and banter went hand in hand with firm yet kind discipline, and Mr. Owen was fun and approachable and his door was always open. You'd often see him playing soccer with the rowdiest boys or lending another teacher a hand. Everyone trusted him. After decades of service, he retired to a cacophony of thanks and well wishes.

Ms. McLaughlin, on the other hand, took a more Victorian approach to her headship of my secondary school. Aloof, unapproachable, out of touch with teenage life in the '80s, and quite formidable, she believed in hard work and not complaining. She terrified me, and we avoided her religiously.

Whether principals, doctors, coaches, police officers, or presidents, the authority figures in our lives shape how we interact with the world, each other, and God. If we've had authoritarian, abusive, aggressive, or controlling experiences, we're more likely to be hesitant about coming to God. No one wants to be belittled, berated, or banished like Adam and Eve when they dare question him. So we back away.

Again, the lie wins. Not until we shift our view of God— from authoritarian, unapproachable, and easily angered, to the humble priest who's not "out of touch with our reality" but willing to kneel at our feet—do we meet our God in human likeness who "experienced it all—all but the sin." Not until then are we ready to "walk right up to him and get what he is so ready to give. *Take* the mercy, accept the help" (Heb. 4:15–16 MSG, emphasis added).

There's no need to hide our questions in embarrassment, fear, or shame. Quite the opposite. We are constantly encouraged to cast them onto him because he loves us (1 Pet. 5:7).

"I can't question God" is another lie fueling the fire keeping us from God. The truth is, our questions don't scare or faze God. They don't make him mad, disappoint him, or cause him to reject us. He knows and loves us anyway, and is more interested in a relationship with us than in our having all the answers. God loves a cheerful doubter, especially one who comes to him with their questions.

Wash All of Me

A Daringly Honest Story of Doubt
Based on John 12:12–13 and 13:3–12

It was the night before Passover, and it had been a wild few days. As Jesus rode into Jerusalem, the crowds had erupted, carpeting the road with palm fronds and cloaks, shouting for their King to rescue them from the clutches of the Romans. But then the mood changed. His mood shifted.

In the upper room, as we were reclining around the table and talking, the meal spread before us, Jesus got up, took off his outer robe, grabbed a towel, and wrapped it around his waist without a word. John looked at me sideways, his brow furrowed, as if to say, *What on earth is Jesus up to?* I shrugged, clueless. Jesus wasn't the most predictable guy at the best of times, and admittedly some of the things he did seemed odd, but he always had a reason and we trusted him, so I kept my mouth shut.

Slowly, he poured clean, cool water into a basin, knelt, cradled John's dusty, crusty, calloused foot in his hand, and gently wiped away the day's dirt. I couldn't believe it. John sat there, hesitant and confused as the fresh, clear water turned brown and murky, but he didn't say a word. None of the guys did. Maybe they liked the intimacy of it, maybe they were willing to let Jesus be his normal, strange self, trusting they'd get to hear his reasoning when he was done. Or perhaps they were too embarrassed or afraid to ask. I don't know. All I know is I was having none of it.

Washing feet is a servant's work. It's lowly, humiliating work. Not something a rabbi should be doing, and certainly not something a coming king should lower himself to.

So as Jesus knelt before me, I challenged him: "Lord, are you going to wash my feet?"

Reassuring me it would soon become clear, he tried again. But I held my ground. I'm as stubborn as I am impulsive.

Yanking my foot away, I shot back, "You're not going to wash my feet—ever!"

Then, as always, he flipped the whole thing on its head—if he didn't wash my feet, I couldn't be part of what he was doing—so you can imagine what I said next: "Master! Not only my feet, then. Wash my hands! Wash my head!" I was all in.

We never did take Jesus up on his suggestion to wash each other's feet, but we do try to be humble servants like he was that night by offering grace to the least deserving, even those with horribly dirty feet.

Now, thirty years later, as I sit in Rome and write to encourage the churches of Asia Minor in their suffering and persecution, I'm reminded of that night. Of course, with all that followed, it's memorable for so many reasons. But Jesus's willingness to lower himself—not just to his knees in front of us, but to humbly take the role of a servant—is a constant reminder of his humility, grace, and approachability.

For any king to do this, let alone the King of Kings, is astonishing. It means we get to approach him with everything we're holding— our worries, burdens, fears, and anxious, whirling thoughts. We get to come to him with our shame, regret, and even our faith-shaking questions. They might be grimy, but he doesn't care.

The churches I'm writing to are struggling with this, and maybe you are too. So I want to remind you of Jesus's approachability. Nothing and no one is stopping us or acting as guard or gatekeeper. We can throw our cares on him once and for all, because he cares for us with such affection.

Remember, my friend, Jesus's door is always open. He's never shocked or outraged by what we want to bring, ask, or even challenge him on. Don't let the lie "I can't question God" keep you away. He wants to kneel at your feet, take your dirt and grime in his hands, and listen. He's making you a part of everything he's doing.

Killing the Lies

The Myth: I can't question God.

The Mantra: God loves a cheerful doubter.

The Reminder: Your questions don't worry God. He knows what's eating you up and loves you whether you're doubt-riddled or doubt-free, and he'll never reject you for daring to ask your unanswered questions. Be encouraged. Don't hide your questions from God in embarrassment or shame; instead, cast them onto him with confidence that he cares for you deeply. With God there are no unaskable questions.

The Reset: This is your time and space to chat with God about it all. Here are a few questions, prompts, and activities to help you give it a go.

- When you think of God, do you have visions of an Aslan/Gandalf figure, or more of the Godfather or President Snow from *The Hunger Games*? What movie or book character do you associate with God? Why do you think that is?

- How has your view of God shaped your willingness to talk to him about what's troubling you?

- Plot where you sit on the grid below, and think about whether you view God's approachability as high or low and whether you have high or low levels of shame, guilt, fear, or embarrassment around your doubts.

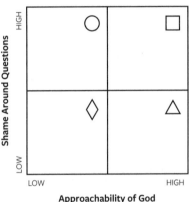

Approachability of God

☐ You see God as approachable but carry some shame, guilt, or nervousness around your questions. Where do you think this has come from? Can you park those emotions at the door when you sit with God? Allow God's approachability to guide you into conversation with him.

△ You don't worry about coming to God, and your questions and doubts don't hold a lot of shame or guilt. You're in a great place to chat with God.

○ You worry God isn't approachable while also carrying shame and guilt around your questions. As we walk through this guide, it's important to do all you can, with God's help, to let go of the lies holding you back and come to him anyway. He loves you.

◊ You might not be carrying a lot of shame or guilt about your questions, but something is making you hesitant to approach God and chat. Is it one of the lies we've explored? How might you let it go and chat to God about all you're holding?

LIE #4: I Can't Tell God *That*

Back in that church with the bare brick walls, another plate of pasta casserole sitting empty on my lap, I listened to the now-familiar speaker in his black jeans and T-shirt. He was inviting us to imagine sitting alone in a movie theater.

He paused, letting the image take hold and the suspense build, before asking us to envision the screen coming to life, opening on a scene with us as a baby bouncing on our mother's hip, then as a toddler biting our little sister with glee. There I was at Christmas, rushing into Granny's arms, then helping her down the path a few years later. As he continued to guide us through this imaginary movie, I grew taller while Gran became frailer. Then there I was at school, ballet, and lacrosse. Cheating on my history test. High school graduation, college hijinks, and the first day of my first job. He told us to imagine someone had followed us through life filming Every. Single. Moment.

As embarrassing as that was, even in the privacy of my own mind, he then asked us to imagine that film we'd just watched had a soundtrack of every thought we'd ever had—every dream we'd longed for, every compassionate prayer, jealous heartache, ugly belief, racial bias, and plan for revenge that had ever floated through our minds. Nothing was to be left out. Gifted in the art of pregnant pauses, he allowed the pleasant surprises, sinking regrets, and horror of our own internal reality (more devastating than I like to admit) sink in throughout the replay.

The goal of this unnerving exercise was to help us connect with the shame and embarrassment of our terrible decisions before inviting us into the grace-filled news of the gospel. It didn't work. However imaginary, sitting through a film of my life with this level of honesty didn't make me want to leap into Jesus's arms. Quite the opposite.

The cringe-worthy feeling of embarrassment and deep shame from the awful things I'd done (and even worse, thought) didn't just vanish in a puff of grace. Horrified to see it all laid out in Technicolor and embarrassed to admit its accuracy, even to myself, I dreaded the idea of God previewing the movie and knowing every little excruciating detail.

The intellectual knowledge of God's grace washing it clean was great in theory, but it didn't stop my heart from plummeting through my new winter boots. God knew. I knew he knew. He knew I knew he knew. The awkward silence stretched between us, goading me to sprint for the door.

Years later, with my growing list of problems with God-FaithChurch, God and I had reached a stalemate again. God knew I had doubts. I knew he knew. He knew I knew he knew. Yet I stood there, too embarrassed and scared to confess, too confused by his role in it all to dare talk to him.

God had called us to plant a church, preach the gospel, and disciple people into more of what he has for them. He'd called me to write and speak and encourage others through hard times. There was even a chapter in my first book encouraging others to be honest with God. Yet there I was, embarrassed, ashamed, even frightened of my questions. The lie had won.

My friend and fellow author Jennifer Dukes Lee says it well: "Honesty feels vulnerable and scary, like walking into a room without pants on."[6] Asking God my big, hairy, potentially faith-destroying questions demanded I walk into his throne room in nothing but my granny-sized Bridget Jones undies to ask him what his deal is. No thanks.

True intimacy with God is tricky for most of us mere mortals. We've either grown up on a diet of holiness and guilt and see God as demanding and vengeful, or we're not ready to admit our deepest thoughts and stand pantless in front of him. Either way, we shy away from getting closer without thinking much about it, reasoning we're close-ish and that's just fine.

Whatever the reason, the myth "I can't (or shouldn't) tell God *that*" reflects our unwillingness to approach God. We know it's a lie, but knowing it's not true and living into the truth are two very different things.

Whether it's on social media, in gossip magazines, or on late-night talk shows, it's hard to miss the encouragement to embrace our whole selves—if we want to *be* whole, we must love and accept the entirety of who we are, including (and often especially) our faults and quirks. For a while, I worried this was either a pink ticket to being our normal, obnoxious selves or it advocated a level of self-reflection bordering on self-obsession. Now I see it differently. If God has embraced all of me, why shouldn't I? If I don't accept my whole self, with my faults and faltering faith, how can I be fully me with myself, God, or anyone else? It's not a free pass to never changing, but it does gift me the courage to show up as I am today.

Embracing honesty and vulnerability is demanding. It feels like work. And the thought of all that soul searching, intimate sharing, and coming face-to-face with God with all my questions and accusations (for that's what many of my doubts had become—accusations) seemed too hard. My default assumption was that I couldn't and shouldn't be honest with God.

But this logic is topsy-turvy. The reality is that God's seen and heard it all before—he already knows my deepest, darkest doubts. God's unshockable, and nothing we say persuades him we're not worth his time.

———— Two Adulterers ————

Daringly Honest Stories of Doubt Based on John 4 and Psalms 13, 22, 42, and 44 (quoted verses in italics)

This woman is well-known (pun totally intended—know who I'm talking about?!). We meet her in the dusty hill town of Sychar as Jesus heads back from Judea to Galilee through Samaria. It's noon, the sun is high, and while the normal hour for fetching water from the town's well has long since passed, she is there as Jesus arrives hot and tired. The familiar story unfolds vividly, with Jesus telling her to fetch her husband and her admitting she has no husband.

Jesus replied, *"You're right! You don't have a husband—for you have had five husbands, and aren't even married to the man you're living with now"* (John 4:17–18 NLT).

If he'd busted me like that—publicly exposing how messed up I am and the details of my failed love life—my anger and embarrassment would have shot back, "How dare you?" But she doesn't toss water in Jesus's face, storm away, or even raise her voice in defiance or shame. She simply leans in, wanting more of whatever God has for her.

A shepherd boy turned king. The man after God's own heart. The adulterer and murderer. If anyone should feel icky talking to God, embarrassed or ashamed by their questions, King David's your man. But despite his doubts and self-induced struggles, he doesn't buy into the lie that he can't or shouldn't tell God. He boldly and unashamedly cries out to God, even at times accusing him. Here are just a few examples from the Psalms to give you a taste.

How long, LORD? Will you forget me forever?
How long will you hide your face from me?
How long must I wrestle with my thoughts
and day after day have sorrow in my heart?

Psalm 13:1–2

My God, my God, why have you forsaken me?
Why are you so far from saving me,
so far from my cries of anguish?
My God, I cry out by day, but you do not answer,
by night, but I find no rest.

Psalm 22:1–2

I say to God my Rock,
"Why have you forgotten me?
Why must I go about mourning,
oppressed by the enemy?"
My bones suffer mortal agony
as my foes taunt me,
saying to me all day long,
"Where is your God?"

Psalm 42:9–10

Awake, Lord! Why do you sleep?
Rouse yourself! Do not reject us forever.
Why do you hide your face
and forget our misery and oppression?

Psalm 44:23–24

Why? Why? Why? How long? David doesn't hold back. He might be an adulterous, murdering screwup you'd hope would feel more than a tinge of embarrassment in the presence of God (especially since he and God have been so close for so long). But he's also a man who knows who God is and who he is to God. He's grounded in the knowledge God knows it all and loves him anyway. So David leans in further and doesn't shy away.

~~~~

These examples tenderly remind us how God leans in closer as we turn towards him, especially when we're brutally honest.

Unlike being forced to watch a movie of your life, God never forces us to share our worries and questions. He won't sit us down and tell us what we already know, shaming us into a confession. He might convict us, but he never shames us. His door is open, but we're the ones who must walk through it.

I like to think that as we come to God with our doubts and questions, he calls us *women after his own heart*, because spending just a few minutes in the Psalms tells us great faith isn't doubt-free faith. Great faith is saying, "I don't get it, God, but I'd rather do life with you than without you. I'm willing to not believe the lie I can't tell you stuff."

> **God isn't after blind faith. He wants more for us and our relationship with him.**

If you've read Bonnie Gamus's novel *Lessons in Chemistry*, you'll know that Rev. David Wakely's wonderful correspondence about faith with the famously difficult and ferociously logical scientist, Calvin Evans, spans many years. In the TV adaptation (not nearly as good as the book), he encourages Calvin to keep asking questions, saying, "People who don't ask questions have blind faith, and blind faith is the furthest thing from faith."[7]

He's right. God isn't after blind faith. He wants more for us and our relationship with him. Nothing delights him more than us leaning into all our questions and confusion with our eyes wide open. He knows what David and the woman at the well may have sensed—that our doubts are our faith's superpower, not its kryptonite.

Some theologians say even Jesus doubted as he knelt in Gethsemane before his crucifixion. Others believe his cry was simply Jesus expressing his sense of abandonment and anguish, highlighting his humanity. Either way, he cried out to God without shame, secrecy, or embarrassment. God knew. Jesus knew God knew. And God knew Jesus knew he knew! Yet still he cried out. He didn't succumb to the lie he couldn't talk to God. As coheirs with Christ, we don't have to either.

Killing the Lies

The Myth: I can't tell God *that*.

The Mantra: There is holiness in my humanity. If adulterers and murderers and even Jesus cry out to God, so can I.

The Reminder: The Bible is full of ranters, ragers, doubters, and skeptics, especially in the Psalms. Here we find permission to be fully us, bringing our joys, pain, confusion, doubts, and complaints to him unhindered, however embarrassed or ashamed we are. Letting it all out to God brings us closer to him as he holds space for who and how we are, really.

The Reset: This is your time and space to chat with God about it all. Here are a few questions, prompts, and activities to help you give it a go.

- Go back a few pages and reread those verses from the Psalms, this time out loud, and imagine you're sitting with Jesus, speaking to him directly. Feel free to switch out David's questions and accusations for your own. How do you imagine Jesus reacting?

- Now read them again, imagining Jesus smiling and cheering as you go through your list.

- Sometimes it's easier to write our prayers to God than say them out loud or in our head. Fill in the gaps of this prayer to make it your own.

Dear God,
Deep down I know I can come to you with
anything, but sometimes it's hard.
Forgive me. The lie that I can't tell you
my doubts has come between us.
I'm sorry.
The question I'm most worried about
asking you is _____.
And the reason I've been so hesitant
to tell you is _____.
So now you know!
I've let it out of the bag. Not that you didn't know already.
Thank you for not turning away or rejecting
me for doubting or being brutally honest.
I love how you love me anyway.
May I feel that love in the moments and days ahead.
Protect me from the enemy's lie that
telling you was a BAD idea.
Give me more of your living water to
quench my doubting thirst.
And may my desire for your closeness always
outweigh my need for understanding.
In the name of your Son, who cried out first.
Amen.

LIE #5: I Have to Choose— Faith *or* Doubt

The dotted humming frog of South America and the Colombian lesserblack tarantula are besties. Or, in scientific lingo, they live symbiotically. Rather than being enemies or one preying on the other, these two creatures have formed an unlikely relationship where both species benefit from living close to each other on an ongoing basis. The frog gains the protection of its big, hairy arachnid friend by setting up home in the tarantula's burrow, and in return it munches on the local carnivorous ants who eat tarantula eggs for breakfast. It's a win-win. Both benefit. Two apparent enemies are better off for each other's company.

Conditioned to assume doubt is parasitic—that it will eventually consume our faith question by question—our go-to response is to kill doubt off before it can kill our faith. But what if doubt and faith live in a mutually beneficial symbiotic relationship instead? There'd be no need to set our doubts on fire like a tick on a dog's back, and they could live happily ever after together, fueling, growing, and strengthening each other. Rather than suffering, our relationship with God would benefit.

In so much of life, we can't have everything, but here we *can*. We don't have to choose. Peter Enns describes his wrestling with questions of faith this way: "While there has been much angst and some pain, there has also been a deepening, a maturation, a growth in my spirit that has led me closer to God."[8]

Some might worry I'm advocating we nurture our doubts, which does, I admit, sound strange and wholly counter to our call to grow in faith and Jesus's call to not doubt but have faith. However, if we hear Jesus's words not as a demanding "do it or else" command but as the loving encouragement of a parent who knows they are trustworthy—even if the child isn't ready to jump into their arms from the climbing frame—we hear God's continuous invitation towards faith and intimacy. And if, at the same time, we shift how we think about our questions and how we phrase them—from negative and accusatory to curious and openhearted and with a growth mindset—we become less defensive, almost welcoming when they show up. Our challenge is to allow our questions to do the work of drawing us deeper into the relationship we're trying to protect in the first place.

Our challenge is to allow our questions to do the work of drawing us deeper into the relationship we're trying to protect in the first place.

Friend, even though it might sometimes feel like it, your doubts aren't the executioner of your faith. Your doubts are its teacher, guide, and coach. The strength of your faith isn't diminished by the strength of your doubts or inversely proportional to them. The strength of your faith is directly proportional to your willingness to embrace your questions and doubt-walk—holding hands with both faith and doubt—in conversation with God. You don't have to choose between faith or doubt, you can and do have both.

---------------------- **The Jump** ----------------------

A Daringly Honest Story of Doubt
Based on Matthew 14 and Mark 6

Are you asking if I've ever doubted Jesus? If during those three wild years I ever questioned who he was, what he was doing, or why and how he was doing it? Or wondered whether I should walk away?

Is the Salt Sea salty? Do the Romans build roads and march in formation? Of course I did!

Looking at me now, all these years later, it's understandable if you assume I'm a man of great faith who never doubts, questions, or wonders what on earth God's up to. You probably see the guy Jesus called "the Rock," but let me assure you, I would never, not then or now, call myself a man of great faith or say I never doubt.

Back when we were traveling around with Jesus, there was a night close to the end of his ministry when I thought my faith was rock solid, but in reality it was as fragile as wet papyrus. The truth is, it's still that way. Let me tell you what happened.

Honestly, I don't know what got into me. It's no secret I'm a wee bit impulsive, and yes, the other guys give me a hard time about it. But when it comes to Jesus, I couldn't get enough. He was and is magnetic. I wanted to be with him, be like him, know him more. I'd do anything for him. Still will.

If he says jump, I'll jump. So that night I did. Out of a boat.

Earlier that morning we'd heard that Herod Antipas had beheaded John the Baptist. We all knew John was in prison, but some of his disciples had come to talk to Jesus just a few days before, so we assumed he was okay. Poor Jesus. We were all in shock, but Jesus took the death of his cousin hard and quietly slipped away in one of the boats to pray. I didn't blame him.

Of course, it didn't take long for word to get out about where he was and for hordes of people to show up as usual. There must have been over five thousand of them. The guy couldn't get a moment's peace. If it had been me, I'd have told everyone to get lost—but of course Jesus didn't. He had pity on them and even healed those who were sick.

Before we knew it, the sun was setting over the lake and people were getting hungry. We suggested they head home for dinner, but once again Jesus had other plans. Somehow, with just five fish and a couple of bread loaves, he fed the entire crowd. We even had leftovers to spare. It was miraculous.

Miracles on that scale blow my mind, and I was still thinking about those twelve baskets of leftovers when we set off in the boat. I was so preoccupied I didn't even notice Jesus wasn't with us. I wished he had been. We're fishermen and can deal with the storms and unpredictable waters of the lake, but the wind whipped up the waves, buffeting the boat something terrible, and we could have done with him calming the storm again.

Then, out of nowhere, in the distance off to one side, we saw a figure walking on the water, coming towards us. We panicked. Despite it being about four in the morning, when the sun should have been making an appearance, it was still pretty dark on the stormy lake, and we thought it was a ghost until we heard a familiar voice. We'd know that voice anywhere.

"Courage, it's me. Don't be afraid."

Jumping up and almost overturning the already rocking boat, I shouted into the wind, "Lord, if it's really you, command me to come to you on the water."

My shout disappeared into the squall, but I had to be sure it was him. I wasn't jumping out of a boat in the middle of a gale for just anyone. Calm as anything, he replied with one simple word: "Come."

That's all it took for me to swing my legs over the boat's gunwale and leap into the water. Or, more accurately, "onto" the water, because as crazy as it sounds, I didn't plunge into its icy depths. My sandals hardly got wet, let alone my tunic. The water was . . . solid.

As I walked towards Jesus, my eyes fixed on his, for a moment I thought, *I'm actually doing this! I'm walking on water!* But then, as I looked down at the churning waves below me, the salty wind startled me back to reality and I began to sink.

As bold and impulsive as I am, it doesn't take much for me to regret my decisions, so without caring how embarrassing it was, I yelled, "Lord, save me!"

In a heartbeat, he grabbed my hand, pulled me up, and asked what got into me. He even called me fainthearted—"you of little faith"—and asked me why I doubted, which was crushing. But at that moment, all I wanted was to get back to the safety of the boat.

Matthew, Mark, and John scooched over, making room for me and my soggy tunic, and then, as soon as Jesus stepped on board they broke out in worship, calling him the Son of God. It was easy for them. They'd watched the whole scene play out from the safety of the boat, but me? I just sat there shivering, beating myself up.

They had faith while I had clearly chosen doubt.

Ever since Jesus called me to follow him, I'd done all I could to please him and grow my faith. I know I didn't always do it brilliantly, but I did my best. All I ever wanted was to be a man of great faith.

Sitting there as the guys praised their hearts out and salt water dripped from my tunic, it seemed like proof I never would be. All I'd be was a man of great doubt. Great faith doesn't doubt. Doubts kill faith. You have to choose—faith or doubt.

Or that's what I thought.

I wish I could go back and tell young Peter not to be so hard on himself. I'd encourage him to keep doing all he can to grow his faith and not believe the lie that it's one or the other. I'd remind him he was the first to have faith that night, not the other disciples. He had enough faith to cry out to Jesus, to get out of the boat, and even to walk on water.

I might be Peter, the Rock, the one Jesus built his church on (and not just any church, mind you, a church so expansive with energy that not even the gates of hell can keep it out), the one he gave full access to the kingdom of God. But I still have my moments.

I don't believe certainty is what Jesus expects or wants from us. Intimacy is. These years have shown me that relationship with us, however messy, confusing, or complicated we find it, is what Jesus longs for. Our doubts don't change that. We can have faith and doubt.

Since you asked, maybe this is what you need to hear too . . .

A rope is made by twisting thin strands of thread together to make a thicker, stronger strand that's then added to other strands and twisted again, over and over until the rope is thick and strong. Ecclesiastes 4:12, which uses the image of "a cord of three strands," is often used at weddings to symbolize the coming together of a bride, groom, and God into a braid that's strong and hard to unravel. We can think of our relationship with God in a similar way. As we weave the strands of our doubt and faith together in constant communication with God, it's like twisting the cord together. Our spiritual formation and walk with God deepen, inevitably drawing us closer to him where our bond isn't easily broken.

When we're feeling lost, we can't just snap our fingers and vanquish our doubts with a silver bullet, but we can befriend them, welcoming them along for the ride. The only condition? They don't get to set our GPS or drive.

Killing the Lies

The Myth: I have to choose—faith *or* doubt.

The Mantra: Walking by faith means doubt-walking with God.

The Reminder: Heroes of the faith like Peter show us that walking by faith isn't walking in certainty. It's not choosing between faith and doubt; it's allowing doubt to fuel our faith in a gloriously mysterious symbiotic relationship that draws us into God's presence as we walk and talk with him.

The Reset: This is your time and space to chat with God about it all. Here are a few questions, prompts, and activities to help you give it a go.

- Take twenty scraps of paper and on ten of them write ten things you love about God, your faith, or the church—one for each piece of paper. On the other ten scraps put ten things you're doubting, confused about, or questioning. Keep the piles separate, taking a moment to reflect on what they represent and mean to you. How important is it to you to keep the piles separate? How would it feel to mix them up together?

- Now mix them up, putting all twenty in a bowl or basket. Holding your bowl of paper scraps, take a moment to quiet yourself and pray the following prayer. As you do, physically place the bowl on a Bible, in front of a cross, or anywhere that can represent placing your doubt-riddled faith and faith-filled doubt into Jesus's arms.

Lord Jesus,
When I had my faith and doubts separated
into two piles, it felt safe.
And honestly, I wish finding peace with it
all was as simple as
sweeping the doubt scraps into the trash.
That would be so much easier.
But here they are, all mixed up together.
This meager basket of faith and doubt is my reality.
Forgive me for believing I have to choose one or the other.

Show me how to place them in your care,
walking and talking with you as I go.
Use my questions to point me to you and draw us closer.
Remind me, Lord, that answers and certainty aren't my goal,
closeness with you is.
You've never asked me to choose.
You call me blessed for believing anyway.
For that, I'm grateful and give you glory.
In your name and as doubtfully as ever,
Amen.

• Take three pieces of thread and braid them into a short cord, then tie it round your wrist. Every time you find yourself worrying about your doubts, rub it between your fingers and remind yourself of Peter and how he had both faith and doubt in the same boat ride.

Curiosity Saves the Cat

Moses is famous for many things. He's the guy who was set afloat in a basket on the River Nile as a baby, was adopted by Pharaoh's daughter, and committed murder before going into hiding and tending sheep. And he's the chap God spoke to from a burning(ish) bush. We remember him challenging Egypt's pharaoh to let the people of Israel go, the ensuing plagues, and the Red Sea parting as the Israelites fled. When someone says the name Moses, images of stone tablets, pillars of cloud and fire, morning manna, and years of wandering through the desert come to mind.

If you've resonated with Moses's lack of eloquence or his hesitancy to follow God's call, then you may call him reluctant, fearful, or relatable. But for the most part, Moses's story conjures words like *faithful*, *resilient*, *compassionate*, *humble*, even *courageous*. But rarely *curious*.

The desert around Mount Horeb is dry and scrubby, and a shepherd's days were tiring, relentless, and lonely. Moses had been tending sheep in this unforgiving landscape for forty years. That's a lot of sheep and even more dust. When a very ordinary bush spontaneously burst into flames yards from where Moses stood, he couldn't not check it out.

Is it on fire? Yes and no. So how are there flames? How did it catch on fire? Why isn't it charring? Curious, wanting to see more, Moses did what no shepherd should ever do—he turned away from his flock.

The story in Exodus 3 is so familiar, we often forget how, at this point, Moses had no idea God was behind the bush's pyrotechnics. Who knows what was going through his mind? Did he have an inkling God was up to something, or was he simply as curious as a kid always asking *why*? It's hard to know, but the story tells us he wondered *why* the bush wasn't being consumed, and this openness to the unexpected and unexplainable was the catalyst to everything that unfolded, eventually leading him to speak to God face-to-face, just like to a friend (see Exod. 33:11).

When God calls to Moses from inside the bush, Moses answers with the Hebrew word *hineni*, which means "I am ready to hear and obey, whatever you ask of me." I'll admit, I'm impressed. If my potted plant burst into flames and called my name while I was cleaning the dishes, I doubt I'd say, "Hey God, I'm here, tell me what you want me to do and you can consider it done." The chances are I'd reach for the nearest fire extinguisher. Despite always aspiring to have the kind of relationship Moses had with God and to be as willing to follow God's call as Moses eventually was, the bar seems too high and my spiritual wherewithal too low.

It's easy to be open to God and willing to follow his call until it seems too painful, divisive, or unfathomable. It's easy to say "Here I am, Lord" until his will rubs salt into the doubts and concerns corroding your faith.

For Moses, like for many of us, it may have been relatively easy to say "I am ready to hear and obey, whatever you ask of me" when he had no clue what God would ask of him. But once he hears God's plan, he has second thoughts and promptly whips his fire extinguisher out and backs away.

"Who am I that I should go to Pharaoh and bring the Israelites out of Egypt?" (Exod. 3:11).

"What if they do not believe me or listen to me?" (4:1).

"Pardon your servant, Lord. I have never been eloquent, neither in the past nor since you have spoken to your servant" (4:10).

Finally, Moses asks the question we all ask eventually: "But why me? What makes you think that I could ever go to Pharaoh and lead the children of Israel out of Egypt?" (3:11 MSG).

Why me, God?

Whether we are being called to endure the unendurable or to do something we feel utterly ill-equipped for, our question is often the same: *Why me, Lord?*

As is often his way, God didn't answer Moses directly. Moses heard no assurance about who he was or why God had chosen him. There was no pep talk about how he was a better orator than he gave himself credit for, or how God would do the persuading on Moses's behalf if the people didn't believe him. And there was no tutting or sighing from God, no admonishment for Moses's audacity to ask questions: *Who are you to question me? I'm God, and you, most certainly, are not.*

No, God's answer was purely his promise: "I will be with you" (4:12).

And he was. God's presence went with Moses through everything, including his grumbling, questioning, defiance, outbursts, and disillusionment.

However much we're struggling with the ways of GodFaithChurch, God makes the same promise to us in the face of our questions: *I will be with you.*

And he is.

What I love about Moses's story is how God's encouragement and promise to be with him doesn't suddenly put a stop to Moses's questions. It's not a silver bullet, vaccine, or miraculous cure for his doubts, curiosity, or questioning. The difference God's promise made to Moses isn't how it quelled his burning questions but how it gifted him a safe place and person to bring them to. At various times in his life, Moses questions God's judgment, God's ways, his own abilities, his people, and even whether God will show up or not, despite witnessing extraordinary miracles and never seeing God renege on a promise or not come through. Still, God is with him.

Moses walked with God through great doubt and great faith. The key isn't whether he questioned, argued, obeyed, followed, or believed God—it's that he was in relationship with God, and at every turn went to God over anything or anyone else.

God told a questioning Moses he'd be with him.

In Matthew 11:28–30, Jesus's invitation for the tired and weary to come to him and his promise that we'll find rest has never excluded the doubters or skeptics burned by religion or life (just read the Beatitudes in Matthew 5 if you don't believe me). Throughout Scripture, God repeats his promise to be with us, and time and again we're invited to go to him no matter how doubt-riddled, fed up, or spiritually beat we are.

What if we took him up on his offer? Even if just for a moment, can we believe he won't leave us? Can we take the weight of everything we're carrying and hand it to him? No topic is taboo to God. There's no baggage off limits, no hurt too painful, no question too silly, no accusation too insulting, no emotion too fiery, no state of mind too fragile.

He. Will. Be. There. He's not going anywhere.

My friend, you've done the hard work of dealing with the lies and assumptions trying to persuade you that God's not the best person to pour your heart out to. You're free to chat with God and take him up on his offer to come to him confident he'll never leave you. No matter how messy, awkward, painful, or confusing your conversations get.

So let's go for it.

Let's chat with God.

PART 3

God, Can We Chat?

A Daringly Honest Pick 'N Mix of Questions

The best bit of advice I ever received
about how to pray was this:
keep it simple, keep it real, keep it up.

—Pete Greig

Just One Man

Late at night and under the cover of an inky sky, Nicodemus, a Pharisee and member of the Jewish ruling council, snuck out to see Jesus. Better to risk the alleys of Jerusalem at midnight than . . . what? The others knowing he was worried they were wrong? Or maybe he didn't want to be seen talking to the man stirring up the crowds and being branded blasphemous. Perhaps he feared something worse: missing what God was doing, even missing *the* Messiah—the shoot of Jesse (Isa. 11:1 NLT), the righteous Branch (Jer. 23:5), Immanuel (Isa. 7:14), the Prince of Peace (Isa. 9:6)—when he might be sitting on the temple steps. We can only imagine what raced through his mind. But what we do know is that by sneaking into the darkness, he found the light.

Like any good Pharisee, Nicodemus knew the Torah and loved and upheld God's laws. But unlike his priestly counterparts, in the midst of the confusion and even fear around who Jesus was and what he was up to, he wasn't closed to what God might be doing in their midst. What set him apart and took him into the shadows of Jerusalem wasn't some fresh, scholarly insight or unique perspective on the hundreds of messianic prophecies. It was his openness. Nicodemus was probably just as baffled and unsure as the others, just as afraid and threatened by the message Jesus was spreading. But despite that, he was willing to step into the new story God seemed to be writing in their midst, stay curious in the face of what he didn't understand, and reach out to God.

For us, there's no need to slink into the night to chat with Jesus. But if we've spent any time in communities where unwavering faith is a badge of honor and doubts are seen as sinful or the devil's work, it can feel like an insurmountable risk to ask questions. Even if it isn't preached directly, many of us unwittingly absorb the idea that believing is good, doubting is bad, and our spiritual growth objective and discipleship journey must always lead to an unsinkable faith.

Despite being fortunate enough to have come to faith in a church that values curiosity and embraces questions as a mark of an alive and active faith, I find my curiosity and openness often run dry and I easily retreat to the status quo.

Nicodemus didn't seem interested in being heard. He simply wanted to listen.

You couldn't go far in Jerusalem without hearing the chatter about Jesus. The marketplaces, the ancient world's equivalent of social media, were humming with it. *Who is he? Did you hear what he said about us, the poor, being blessed? Did you see him heal the blind man or the guy lowered through the roof? I heard a woman was cured from twelve years of bleeding just by touching him. Do you think God sent him? Could he be the one the prophets spoke of?*

Everyone knew. Everyone was asking the same questions. But only Nicodemus risked everything to go to Jesus with a humble willingness to enter a new story—one he didn't yet understand.

According to John's account of their meeting, Nicodemus didn't lead with a question. His conversation starter with Jesus was a simple statement of what he and the rest of the Pharisees knew so far. "Rabbi, we know that you are a teacher who has come from God. For no one could perform the signs you are doing if God were not with him" (John 3:2).

How Nicodemus didn't verbally vomit all his pent-up questions I have no idea. If I'd snuck into the night and managed to get Jesus alone, away from the crowds and prying eyes of my fellow Pharisees, I'd have unraveled a list of questions as long as a toilet roll and peppered the poor fellow until the rooster crowed. But Nicodemus didn't seem interested in being heard. He simply wanted to listen.

Why Chat with God?

This is where the fun begins, my friend. We've taken time to reframe how we see our doubts and questions, and we've begun to recognize them as not just a normal part of our faith but an important, powerful one with the potential to grow our relationship with God. The myths standing in the way of us coming to God with our questions have been busted wide open, paving the way for us to come with anything and everything on our minds. All that's left is for us to chat with God.

If you're after concrete theological answers, you won't find them here. By all means, grab a theologian and buy them a coffee. Preferably at Starbucks so you can enjoy hearing the barista struggle to call their unpronounceable name, which seems to be a prerequisite for great theological minds: *Hegesippus! Zwingli! Wynkoop! Bonhoeffer!* Then don't let them leave until you've satisfactorily pummeled them with questions.

Please know I'm not advocating theological or biblical illiteracy or ignorance in favor of a quick chat with Jesus. I'm the first to say God speaks primarily through Scripture. But without prayerfully talking to God in our struggles and discerning what he might be saying, we miss an integral part of the puzzle. The study of theology has been invaluable in my life and faith. It has grown and strengthened my love and understanding of the

Lord and helped me navigate difficult seasons with their accompanying questions. But there is not simply one unified theology accepted by all of Christianity. There are many different schools of theology depending on the branch of the church, all of whom believe they have the correct one. Theology alone, without God's input, has always left me wanting more.

Without prayerfully talking to God in our struggles, we miss an integral part of the puzzle.

The "more" I've craved isn't intellectual rigor, historical context, or someone else's point of view. What I actually crave is more closeness with God, a new story about old questions, and a personal guide through the doubts and stories I tell myself when I'm disillusioned and doubting. Which is why we're chatting with God and not N. T. Wright or our local pastor.

Our goal is to grow closer to God one doubt at a time and to find intimacy where answers aren't clear-cut. It's to develop wisdom, trust, faith, and discernment as we walk out our faith in partnership with God. And the only way to do that is, like Nicodemus, to walk and talk with Jesus through the mystery—willing, humble, and open to having him rewrite our doubt stories.

God never promised to give us all the answers. He never promised to share the reason for the heartbreaking, doubt-inducing things that happen. He never promised we'd understand him—not even once we've walked through those pearly gates and been given our proverbial harps and halos.

The one thing God promises time and again is to be with us. Always.

Your Chatting with God Guide

If you've been hoping this part is a Q&A with me or God, I'm afraid you might be disappointed. I wish I could tell you this is your Dorothy moment, when you finally get your minute with the wizard and all will be revealed, but I can't.

What I can promise you is that when we follow Nicodemus's lead and take what we've learned from God's Word into God's presence, listening for what he has for us in our questioning, we always find him.

Most of us want God to rewrite our doubt stories. We want to grow closer to him and are even willing to live with a little mystery, but we're not sure how. We might try journaling our prayers or talking it through with a wise, trusted friend. We might ask for prayer from safe people at church or read stories of people who've come through seasons of doubt stronger and more in love with Jesus than ever. These are all valuable things to do and, in their own way, they've helped me enormously. But this scattergun approach is just that—scattered—and when our faith feels scattered and battered and we're struggling with faith-shame or spiritual disillusionment, the last thing we need is a haphazard, hit-or-miss checklist of options to try.

What we need is a guide, a set of trail blazes marking the way through the dense forest of our confusion. We need a clear, step-by-step, proven practice/rhythm/path—call it whatever you like—with questions, prompts, and prayers to show us the way.

In his book *How to Pray*, Pete Greig, who describes himself as the bewildered founder of the 24/7 Prayer movement, shares how one of his sons, when he heard he was writing a book about how to pray, said, "But that's easy. You just say, 'Dear God,' chat to him for a bit, and then say, 'Amen.'"[1] On the one hand, young master Greig nails it. And as his dad goes on to admit, we often overcomplicate prayer. However, it can be helpful to have a framework to guide our chats. Not to complicate them, but to offer simplicity, direction, and purpose to keep us on track.

> **What we need is a guide, a set of trail blazes marking the way through the dense forest of our confusion.**

About thirty years ago, when I was such a new believer I was still figuring out where the church loo was (yes, loo singular—given many English churches were built in the Middle Ages and lack toilets, this one was a luxury) and wondering if God was serious about loving me, I heard a woman talk about how God had called her to India. Telling the story interview style with our vicar, she recalled how God had said this and she'd responded that. How God had badgered her until she took him seriously, and finally she'd headed off into his call. I sat there stunned. Was she on the phone with God? Having tea with him? Sending telegrams or carrier pigeons? I had no idea. All I knew was that she seemed to have God on speed dial, could hear him as clearly as Charlie hears me open his treat jar from a mile away, and she was confident he'd spoken and it wasn't just wishful thinking or indigestion.

Having a direct line to God would be really handy in a pickle—but more than that, it would be an intimate lifeline.

I wanted what she had, but I was highly skeptical, my phony-ometer on high alert.

The trouble is, chatting to God isn't as easy as it sounds. Most of us get tripped up in some way around the idea of prayer. *How are we meant to do it? When? Where? What's a "good" prayer? What words should we use? Can we pray for anything at all? Will God even listen?* It leaves us hesitant to reach out to God. But our bigger concern is whether we can hear God's reply. Our problem rarely is believing God speaks, but rather knowing *how* to hear him.

Enter the CHAT Conversation Guide.

Leaning heavily on both therapy and spiritual direction traditions, think of this guide as part Cognitive Behavioral Therapy (CBT), part spiritual direction, part guided prayer journal, and 100 percent your opportunity to hold nothing back. It's a place to be ruthlessly honest with yourself and God.

When we use CBT to explore our doubts and faith in partnership with God, drawing on CBT's core idea that our thoughts and perceptions influence our behavior, it helps us become more self-aware. We begin to recognize both the stories we've been part of and the stories we've told ourselves before reflecting on our thoughts and emotions. As we do so, we become increasingly open to the new story God is writing. We get to engage in a reflective dialogue with God, processing where we are in our faith, what's holding us back or tearing us apart, and how we feel about God. Intimacy, not answers, is our sole destination.[2]

Over the rest of this book, you'll find some of the most commonly asked questions we have when we struggle in our faith. Each one follows the same pattern, ending with the CHAT Conversation Guide and a short blessing or prayer. The idea is for this guided format to become part of your conversational prayer rhythm with God. That may sound fancy, but it just means that over time the self-reflection, questions, prompts, and back-and-forth between you and God will grow more familiar, even second nature, enabling you to take them into your everyday conversations with God once you put the book down.

I have a confession. This is the part of a book I tend to either skip or skim through the questions with a perfunctory nod before rushing into my day. I arrogantly assume I'll get what I need from thinking the prompts through as Charlie and I take our evening stroll, claiming "I'm not a big journaler" as my excuse. For folks like me, we miss out. The slower, more intentional act of letting our thoughts flow on paper helps us figure out what we're *really* thinking and feeling and dig a bit deeper than we'd take ourselves if left to our own devices. We're also left with the gift of a tangible record to reflect back on how far we've come and grown with God.

There is space in every conversation to go deeper if you wish, so please don't feel confined by my prompts. Feel free to make them your own. This is for you and God.

Paul tells us to "be transformed by the renewing of your mind" (Rom. 12:2), but that's not as easy as it sounds. If it's deciding what to wear for a girls' night out, my mind "renews" a hundred times before my mascara's dry. But when it comes to the way I think, feel, and act towards myself and God on a deeper level, it renews as fast as a herd of tortoises on Nyquil. This section is the help we need, the guided invitation to chat and partner with God, so we can let him do the heavy lifting of transformation as we listen and follow his lead.

To keep it super simple and memorable, I've used the acrostic CHAT to guide our conversations with God. CHAT stands for:

Consider the Facts
Honor the Story You're Telling Yourself
Ask God What He Has to Say
Team **U**p with God Moving Forward

Consider the Facts

No matter how long we've lived, how bright and breezily we've sailed through life, or how hard and devastating our path has been, there's always more than one story to be told—the story of the unfolding events as well as the resulting emotional and spiritual stories. To pin down where our doubt began, we start with what happened and how we came to be asking the question we're holding. This is the tangible, objective, journalist's view of the events and circumstances that have led us here. Just the facts, ma'am!

At this stage, we keep it clear of what we thought, how we felt, who's wrong and who's right, the pain it has caused, and the bitterness we hold. Our inner critic or defense lawyer definitely doesn't get to narrate this one. This is a story everyone can agree on.

For Nicodemus the facts were clear: There was a new rabbi in town. The people claimed he was performing miracles, some of which Nicodemus had seen for himself. The rabbi claimed to forgive sins.

Everyone agreed on this set of facts.

As we too consider the facts and lay out the story of what brought us to these questions, we can clear away the more subjective, intangible elements of the story and see it stripped of all the emotions we shroud it in. Despite their apparent simplicity, these bare-story bones are anything but straightforward or easy, and they play an irreplaceable role in how our view of God is shaped.

When we look at the factual story of what happened to bring our particular question to the surface, we offer ourselves the gift of acknowledging our hard stories, bringing them to God in their indisputable facts, and seeing them in the raw light of day with God at our side.

Honor the Story You're Telling Yourself

Our minds, in their continuous quest for meaning, calm, and safety, create a narrative out of millions of stimuli, events, and daily inputs.[3] When we give our brains a story, they reward us with calm. Like a puppy who'll happily chew your new Jimmy Choos or a dollar store dog toy, they don't care if the story is based in reality or not—they simply want calm and meaning restored.

Inspired by a piece in Brené Brown's book *Rising Strong* and the work she's done around the story we tell ourselves, I began to see this play out in my life.

Al and I had had a bear of a week. I'd been getting up early to work my tail off on a project that was tanking. Al's dad was sick in the UK, and the dog had puked on the new cream carpet. We had friends coming for dinner, the fridge was as bare as Mother Hubbard's cupboard, and Charlie was crossing his legs because he hadn't been walked.

As Al poured puppy chow into Charlie's bowl, he sighed. "The poor guy hasn't had a walk in ages."

I snapped back, "You can walk him too, you know. I'm not the only one who can do it."

As I'm prone to do, I'd turned his comment into a story of how I'm unreliable and disorganized and failing at everything—work, marriage, friendship, hosting, and even being a half-decent dog mum. This, not the events that actually happened, was the story I was telling myself.

It's this inner narrative—this story behind the story we tell ourselves when we're in pain, things are chaotic, or we feel threatened—that we live by. It shapes everything, from our beliefs to our actions to our relationship with God.

Unlike the factual story of what happened—we were both tired, things weren't going as we'd hoped, and the dog needed some love—we fictionalize it to protect ourselves from the hard feelings we'd rather not feel: *I just can't hold it all together. The project's going to go down the tubes. I'm just not organized enough to be spread so thin. I'm a screwup and Al's blaming me for not looking after Charlie.*

Getting mad at and blaming Al, God, or whoever else happens to be nearby is easier than feeling vulnerable or admitting I'm struggling. My "I'm a screwup" story was an easier and more familiar story than the truth.

Rabbi Rami Shapiro notes how "the stories we tell ourselves about ourselves determine the quality of the selves we imagine we are. The stories we tell about others [including God], determine the quality of our relationships with them."[4]

No matter how easy you find it to name and honor your feelings, thinking about what your body is doing can help you forage for more hidden emotions. Is it tied up in knots? Is your blood boiling? Do you want to shrink away or hit something? Pay attention to what your emotions make you want to do—like devour the cookie jar, leave the room, or go back to bed.

> **We are children of God, created in his image, and our emotions are part of who we are.**

If you're someone who's been told your emotions can't be trusted, are sinful, cloud your reason, should be controlled if you want to be holy, or simply aren't valid, I want to reassure you your feelings matter and are important to God. We are children of God, created in his image, and our emotions are part of who we are. Even Jesus felt big emotions like anger, grief, compassion, and joy. Our emotional capacity is a reflection of God's nature within us.

Many of us adopt negative stories into our thinking and actions. Like a vinyl record stuck in its groove, they keep repeating over and over. Stories like:

I'm not good enough.
I'm too much.

I have to hold it together.
I can't let anyone down.
It's probably my fault.

When we bring these patterns and stories to God and into the light, we begin to recognize them with increasing familiarity. This enables us to start the work of partnering with him to challenge them and hear his story for us.

As we do, we're able to move forward through prayer, reliance on the Holy Spirit, and the application of scriptural truths. We can then navigate and respond better to our emotions and find the wisdom, discernment, and intimacy we're after.

Ask God What He Has to Say

The journey of meaningful change starts as we grapple with our thoughts and emotions and interrogate these broken-record stories to see whether or not they hold water. Thankfully, we don't have to do this alone. We have the ultimate friend, the Holy Spirit, as our champion, spokesperson, burden-bearer, guide, mentor, comforter, helper, and counselor (John 14:16). He knows the facts of what happened and the inaccurate, critical, illogical stories we tell ourselves—and loves us anyway.

Of course, we were there in the room where it happened (*Hamilton*, anyone?), and we know the facts of the story all too well. We've dug into the narrative we made up to make sense of it all. But what we still desperately need is God's perspective. How does *he* see what happened? What does *he* have to say to us about it? What would *he* say to us as a friend? What does *he* want us to know?

In the Old Testament book of Job, it's clear that Job knew the facts: He'd lost his children, livelihood, and reputation, and was now covered in painful sores. He knew the story he was telling himself, and I imagine him sitting in the ashes, scraping his sores with a broken piece of pottery (Job 2:8) as this story played on repeat: "I'm righteous before God. I haven't done anything wrong. God's fallen asleep at the wheel, and because of this divine neglect I'm suffering unjustly." What he was missing—and what he needed more than anything—was God's perspective. So he went and asked for it.

By asking God how he sees the situation or what he has to say in our stories, we begin to unravel the narratives, frustrations, and disillusionment that keep us stuck, and we start the journey of walking with God through the unknowns of life.

Like David, we can ask God to take us by the hand, show us and teach us his ways, and lead us down the path of truth (Ps. 25:4–5). Like Job, we can ask God what he has to say to us. In doing so, we glimpse what we're unable to see alone—God's perspective on our story.

God might want to say more than my prompts give space for, so if a thought, image, Scripture, or memory comes to mind, take a moment to freewrite about it or meditate on it. Ask him to guide you, always remembering how safe, loved, and seen you are when you're together.

Team Up with God Moving Forward

For the most part, we humans are by nature pretty self-focused creatures. Our brokenness is on full display morning, noon, and night in the 24-hour news cycle. We protect our interests, do what makes us feel good, and gratify our own desires over those of God and others. We go to great lengths to minimize discomfort and tend to opt for the easier route if given the choice. I do, anyway. Living with doubts and uncertainty is itchy and uncomfortable, and I don't particularly like it.

"Ants in the pants" of our faith leaves us reaching for the calamine lotion of quick fixes, Instagram platitudes, spiritual sound bites, or entrenched dogma that promises to scratch the itch, calm things down, keep things going, or maintain appearances. Unwilling to risk another run-in with those pesky insects, we risk crafting God in our own image, following our own opinions and beliefs, or walking away altogether.

This is why walking with God in active companionship isn't just *a* way to keep our faith alive or fuel our friendship with God. It's the *only* way I've found to do the often uncomfortable work of self-reflection and formation. We simply can't do it alone. Without the guts, know-how, insight, strength, or (dare I say it) desire, I for one am left randomly swatting at ants—frustratingly lost and running out of spiritual steam. Teaming up with God and walking by the Spirit—letting ourselves be guided, led, counseled, corrected, comforted, fueled, and unconditionally loved through the all-you-can-eat buffet of questions and frustrations we carry—is the only way we can experience the full life God has for us without trying to *be* God.

Let's go to Jesus openly, humbly, willingly, and curiously, and admit: *I don't get it, God. Maybe I never will. But I'm with you, and I know you are with me. I trust you, however shakily, so let's do this.*

Chatting with God . . . About It ALL

▨ God, church just feels hard right now.

It's been two years, God. Two years since we stepped down from pastoring, and we still haven't found a church to call home. We've shopped around (I know, I know, church isn't a used car!), looking for where we fit, where we feel called, where we're led by your presence and can give back and build community. But it's not happening, Lord.

～

For some of us, when church is a struggle, pinpointing exactly *why* might not be easy. For others, our sense of unease or pain can be traced back to a specific moment or series of wounding events. Maybe it was all the comments, squabbling, and political wrangling bulldozing through our church doors over the last few years, leaving rubble in its wake. Or perhaps you're one of the devastatingly high number of people who've been spiritually manipulated, put down, or abused by the church. If you are, I'm so, so sorry.

Whatever brought you to this place, church feels hard. Finding a church home or knowing whether to stay or leave a church is exhausting, and we end up wondering whether we can be bothered with it at all.

We know God's heart for his church—both the big-C global Church and the little-c local church—is to be united, love and serve the world, build one another up, and be a safe place of communal worship.

We know the theory: the church is made up of humans, and we humans are a broken bunch of folks, so church will always be woefully flawed, often lacking, and a deeply frustrating place.

We get the point. But it doesn't change the facts or ease the struggle. So, we go anyway and suck it up—or not—before giving ourselves a hard time. We tell our disillusioned selves we "should" go, and even want to want to go. But the effort feels all too much.

We yearn for the church to be what we know it *can* be because it's often beautiful—full of love, acceptance, healing, spiritual growth, and transformation—a place to belong.

Churches we long to be part of feel like home, where the front door's always open, the kettle's on for tea, and there's a place set at the table for us. Where the conversation always brings us back to who and whose we are and the plans God has for us. It's a place where worries are shared, burdens are carried, and God sits amongst us. The fire in the hearth burns warm and bright.

How do we stay in a church that feels like work? How do we find a church to call home when church feels hard? Do we really need to go to church if we feel closest to God when tending our tomatoes or absorbed in our art? Does God care? And why has he let his church become such a mess?

Such great questions. Let's chat with God.

God, Can We Chat?

Consider the Facts

What specific incident(s) has caused you to ask this question? (Just the facts, ma'am!)

- When you're getting ready for church, what makes you want to stay home instead? The more specific you get, the better.

- If you're not part of a faith community right now but used to be, what was the moment or series of events that caused you to walk away?

- When you're in church—either one you're visiting or your current church home—what makes you feel at home? What makes you want to leave?

- If you've ever been part of a church you love, what about it made you feel this way?

- Where do you (1) feel most connected to God and (2) get to share your gifts with others?

Honor the Story You're Telling Yourself

Get curious about your emotions and inner narrative around this question. In the following exercises, use this prompt: *The story I'm telling myself is . . .*

- Imagine you're walking through the doors of a church. What's the soundtrack (the story you're telling yourself) playing in your mind? Is it about you or God?

- What corners of this question feel too hard to peer into? Why might that be? What's the fear or story going through your mind as you think about taking a look?

Ask God What He Has to Say

Prayerfully ask God to show you how he sees things, including you, and what he might want to say to you as a friend today.

- Where are you in my question, God?

- What, if anything, are you asking me to leave behind with you?

- Who, if anyone, are you asking me to forgive or let go of any bitterness towards?

- How might you be offering me grace or courage in this season?

Team Up with God Moving Forward

As you walk through daily life and face its inevitable frustrations, fears, and doubts, how can you intentionally link arms with God and doubt-walk through your unanswered questions?

- How might God be offering to walk with you into church—either a new community or an old one?

- In what specific ways can you lean on God when it comes to this question?

- What would God's strength and comfort tangibly look like as you go back to church? Ask him to provide what you need.

- What unanswered questions or mystery is God asking you to sit with when it comes to his church?

Lord, your church is beautiful, but it's so terribly broken.
Your bride can be gracious and welcoming, catty and spiteful,
healing and welcoming, abusive and divisive.
It's left me hurt, worn out, and wondering
if it's worth the bother.
Help me find peace in your place,
and enough healing to want to return,
stay, or simply not give up.
Show me the way home to you without needing answers.
Amen.

Chat Notes

■ God, you feel so far away.

It's been one of those weeks. Months if I'm honest, Lord. The anxiety of a looming annual scan appointment has wrestled with back-to-back coaching sessions and a limping dog who can't go much longer without a vet visit. One kid is sick and asking to go to Urgent Care, despite her expired college health insurance, and Al's father has been admitted to hospital four thousand miles away. I know nothing's devastating, but it's still a lot. No heartbreak, but even so . . . it's exhausting.

No matter how hard I've tried to lean on you and trust you through it, God, I'm fading. You feel like a distant star, a pin-prick in the night sky, piercing the inky darkness from light-years away. Beautiful to look at yet too small and unreachable to light my way or warm my cooling heart.

God can feel distant in a heartbeat. One moment he feels close, and together we can handle anything life chucks our way. Then—*poof!*—it's as if he's vanished. In our heads, we know he hasn't nipped off to make a cup of tea, help someone more spiritual, or fallen asleep on the job, but the chill where his warmth once was screams otherwise. At other times, God fades sloth-like into the distance, disappearing over the horizon with casual ease, and we hardly notice his going.

When God feels far off, our untethered souls long for their anchor. We don't like floating in spiritual outer space with just a thin safety line connecting us to our God. That's not how we were created. When God seems distant, his love, comfort, and peace feel further still. Finding his strength is harder than normal, discerning his wisdom more complex, and knowing we're okay almost impossible.

140

Does your logic flow something like this? *Jesus said he loves me, he told me he's with me, but I just can't feel him. How do I know he's with me if I can't feel him? He's obviously not here—either he's not real or, more likely, he's not bothering with me, which is probably my fault. Or maybe both.*

Mine does. We've somehow picked up the belief that as followers of Jesus we *should* be able to feel God with us 24/7, and if we can't, it means he's not there. Jesus tells us to come to him when we're weary and heavy laden, but what happens when we try and feel nothing?

We're left asking, *Where are you God? Are you there or not? I can't do this alone. Are you even real or are you ignoring me? Why can't I feel your comfort and peace? Where's the rest you promise when I come to you running on fumes?* When we're also feeling disconnected from people who matter to us, this can turn into the perfect loneliness storm.

Remembering we're not the first ones to feel far from God can help, and we find solidarity in the Psalms: "Why, LORD, do you stand far off?" (10:1). "LORD, do not forsake me; do not be far from me, my God. Come quickly to help me, my Lord and my Savior" (38:21–22). If only solidarity fixed things.

We happily encourage others that God is close to them because we know it to be inherently true; it's who he is after all—Immanuel, God with us. But when we are the ones feeling cold and alone, distant from the God who's been our constant Shepherd, it feels different. Maybe we're the exception?

But are we? How can we know for sure God is near? How can we feel his presence again? Do we need to sense his presence to know we're loved or to cope and heal from the painful parts of our story? Where is he?

Great questions. Let's chat with God.

God, Can We Chat?

Consider the Facts

What specific incident(s) has caused you to ask this question? (Just the facts, ma'am!)

- When was the last time you felt God's closeness?

- What does God's presence feel like to you?

- Has God's closeness lessened over time or in an instant?

- If a particular event or conversation has left you feeling far from God, what was it? What happened?

Honor the Story You're Telling Yourself

Get curious about your emotions and inner narrative around this question. In the following exercises, use this prompt: *The story I'm telling myself is . . .*

- How does your body react when you imagine the distance between you and God?

- Why do you think God seems far off?

- How does this change the way you feel about him?

- Has it damaged how you feel about yourself? If so, how exactly?

- Do you worry that the way God feels about you has changed? If so, how?

Ask God What He Has to Say

Prayerfully ask God to show you how he sees things, including you, and what he might want to say to you as a friend today.

- God, do you believe the story I'm telling myself? If not, why not?

- When you seem far off, how do you feel about me?

- If we had tea together, what would you want to say to me as a friend?

- Jesus, what do I need to know or hear from you?

Team Up with God Moving Forward

As you walk through daily life and face its inevitable frustrations, questions, and doubts, how can you intentionally link arms with God and doubt-walk through your unanswered questions?

- What might walking with God look like when you don't tangibly feel him beside you?

- How can you lean into him when you're unsure he's next to you?

- What level of disconnection are you okay with as you walk through life?

- Ask God to help you see and feel him in new ways and be content in the mystery of his presence.

God of hugs, high fives, and being held,
the breath of life, Immanuel, the one
who promises endless nearness,
show me your closeness.
In the mystery of your presence,
may I know your arms surround me, your strength fuels me,
and your love is within me,
even if I can't feel it, touch it, see it, or hear it.
Amen.

Chat Notes

■ God, are you even listening?

When Mum was dying, Lord, I prayed for healing. And got nothing.

As my sister, Jo, fought the cancer, I begged for her life. Again, silence.

And despite my constant asking, I still haven't heard a definitive "go for it" on this book, even as it goes off to print.

Is the heavenly playlist turned up too loud? Are all your angels drowning out our prayers, or have you shut the door on me, desperate for some peace and quiet?

Can't you hear us? Are you even listening? What's the deal, Lord?

There are times when the pain surges forward, the direction seems clouded, or our cries for help and healing echo back in hollow silence. We stand with our hands on our hips, chin tilted to the sky, one part mad and one part sad, convinced God's got earplugs in.

When the Shepherd doesn't appear to hear his flock, all trouble breaks loose. Sheep wander off, lions pick off weaklings, the injured and hurt go untended, and the last thing other shepherdless sheep want to do is join his herd. Why would they?

If you feel like you've been screaming into a megaphone—asking, seeking, knocking, over and over as Jesus told us to—but God's on mute with his Do Not Disturb sign tacked to his door, it's little comfort to know you're in good company. But once again, we are.

Speaking on God's behalf, Isaiah assured us God hears our prayers even before we get to "Amen" (Isa. 65:24). Yet David, doubled up in pain, calls to God night and day and hears nothing (Ps. 22:2). If "the man after God's own heart" thinks God's not listening, what chances do normal folks like us have?

What's going on? Is God listening, or isn't he? Why doesn't he answer? Or if he does hear our prayers, what's with the silent treatment? Are we missing something he's trying to teach us?

Great questions. Let's chat with God.

God, Can We Chat?

Consider the Facts

What specific incident(s) has caused you to ask this question? (Just the facts, ma'am!)

- What's brought you to the conclusion that God's not listening to you?

- Have you always felt this way, or has something changed?

- If so, what changed? Be specific.

Honor the Story You're Telling Yourself

Get curious about your emotions and inner narrative around this question. In the following exercises, use this prompt: *The story I'm telling myself is . . .*

- Brain dump every emotion and feeling this question (and how you got here) brings up.

- Do you see a pattern or story emerging?

- What about God's silence scares, annoys, frustrates, or worries you?

- What's communication between you and God normally like?

- What's the story you've made up about you and God?

Ask God What He Has to Say

Prayerfully ask God to show you how he sees things, including you, and what he might want to say to you as a friend today.

- Write a note to God telling him what's happened and the story about yourself and him that you've adopted as truth.

- Now prayerfully write a note to yourself as if it's from God. Try not to overthink it. Simply start with "Dear [your name], this is God . . ." and keep going with what he might be saying to you, even through his silence. As you write, if words, images, or Scriptures come to mind, articulate what God might be saying to you through them.

Team Up with God Moving Forward

As you walk through daily life and face its inevitable frustrations, questions, and doubts, how can you intentionally link arms with God and doubt-walk through your unanswered questions?

- As you walk with God in silence, what might he be asking you to shift, leave, give up, repeat, hold on to, or let go of? If you need his help to do what he's suggesting, ask him to provide it.

- How have you seen God already working in this question even if he still seems silent?

- What reassurance do you have from the Bible that God is listening?

A Blessing in the Silence

May the thunderous silence greeting your prayers,
and the urge it creates to shake God awake,
bring you comfort, not confusion, and
calm your chattering chaos.
Whether you get still and small or fidgety and chatty,
may his still small voice begin to crescendo
that you might know his loving nearness, come what may.

Chat Notes

▣ God, some Bible stories don't sit well.

Genocide, war crimes, full-scale slaughter—not to mention plagues, pestilence, drownings, fratricide (brothers killing their brothers), and filicide (parents murdering their kids). It's all there, Lord, in the black-and-white pages of your book.

Let's not forget the scientifically impossible—the sun standing still in the noonday sky, the entire earth flooding, talking donkeys, never-ending jars of flour, walking on water, and the dead being raised. What's going on with those?

God, is it allegory or exaggeration? Or maybe the Old Testament authors got their facts confused or simply spun a good tale. Did the Israelites kill everyone or leave a few survivors like some commentators say?

If I'm honest, God, some Bible stories—no wait, make that a lot of Bible stories—really don't sit well with me or make sense.

—

When stories in Scripture bring us up short and we can no longer read them with our usual faith-filled confidence, trusting God's got his reasons—which are supposed to be good, after all—they wedge like bitter pills we struggle to swallow.

But the pill is stuck. Slaughter is slaughter no matter how many people you spare.

We know we're not privy to God's ways, and we're grateful his ways aren't our ways, yet sometimes we wish they were. We'd never act so callously. We'd never willfully command the death of thousands (even if they aren't our chosen people), or watch as our people are enslaved and beaten. Or we hope we wouldn't.

But God did. Or that's what it looks like from where we're sitting.

Maybe we should stick to the New Testament stories of love conquering all, of forgiveness, healing, resurrection, and being filled with his Spirit. Even if the stories don't always make sense, they slide down more easily than those a few pages back.

It's hard to trust you, God, when our Bibles appear stained with the blood of the innocent (and I'm not talking about Jesus's). What were you thinking, God? How could you do this? What do these stories of vengeful retaliation and slaughter say about you? Or about me, my children, and those who don't know you?

Great questions. Let's chat with God.

God, Can We Chat?

Consider the Facts

What specific incident(s) has caused you to ask this question? (Just the facts, ma'am!)

- What specific stories or ideas in the Bible do you struggle with most?

- What is it that makes you uncomfortable, angry, or confused about them?

- What messaging around these stories have you heard that has sat uncomfortably with you?

Honor the Story You're Telling Yourself

Get curious about your emotions and inner narrative around this question. In the following exercises, use this prompt: *The story I'm telling myself is . . .*

- How do these struggles with the Bible make you feel about God? About yourself?

- How has the way you feel about God changed because of these stories?

- What might your life look like if you didn't struggle with Scripture?

Ask God What He Has to Say

Prayerfully ask God to show you how he sees things, including you, and what he might want to say to you as a friend today.

- Write Jesus a note (think of it as a psalm or a lament) and tell him your concerns before listening to his reaction.

- Ask God if he's really as _____ (choose your own adjective: judgmental, ruthless, etc.) as you fear.

- Ask God what he has to offer you in this place.

Team Up with God Moving Forward

As you walk through daily life and face its inevitable frustrations, questions, and doubts, how can you intentionally link arms with God and doubt-walk through your unanswered questions?

- Find a big leaf from outside or one of your potted plants, write your fears and concerns about the Bible on it with a marker, and set it free somewhere as an offering to God. Then walk away, leaving those questions with him.

- How might God be asking you to respond to these concerns? A few ideas would be to join a Bible study, pray with a trusted friend, find a spiritual director, go to seminary, walk in the woods.

I don't get it, God.
Bloodshed, violence, revenge—
so out of character for the God of love.
I don't get it, God.
You made the heavens, the cosmos,
millipedes, and manta rays.
Who am I to know your ways?
I don't get it, God. .
Your love for me knows no bounds and
isn't dented by my confusion,
so may I respond in kind and love you
more, even as I understand you less.
Amen.

Chat Notes

▣ God, your people say the most hateful things.

Lord, have you seen the cartoon where there's a chap standing in front of Saint Peter at the pearly gates? Saint Peter—halo shining, quill poised, ready to check the guy in—says, "You were a believer, yes. But you skipped the not-being-a-jerk-about-it part."[5] It's funny because unfortunately it's true. We Christians, your people, can be jerks about our beliefs and how we live them out.

Lord, as election campaigns roar into life, people are getting heated, opinionated, and politically aggressive, and tensions are rising. I hate to say it, but it's often the more hardline Christians leading the way.

Why do your people say the most hateful things?

These hurtful words aren't confined to online forums, the media, or radical sites. Ask your refugee neighbors, members of the LGBTQ community, or friends of color if they've ever been on the receiving end of painful comments from people professing their love of Jesus and the Bible, and you'll hear plenty of stories of scorn, prejudice, hate, rejection, and judgment. Maybe you've been on the receiving end of some of these yourself, and I'm sorry if you have.

Christians and the church are known more for what we're against than what we stand for, and increasingly for how we share those views. It's not a new, twenty-first-century problem, but that doesn't make the hurt any less painful or the comments any less cutting.

As Carey Nieuwhof so rightly notes, nonbelievers are put off not because they *don't* know any Christians but because they *do*,[6] and now this is turning many believers into doubting believers.

If you've ventured to voice your frustrations and concerns about the hateful, harmful things you've heard believers say, you may have been met by a barrage of reasons or excuses. Are we misunderstood? Sure. Do we have an image problem? Definitely. But for those outside the church (and increasingly for those of us within it), the more pressing issue is our love and compassion—or lack of it.

Why do your people say such hateful things, God? Why are some believers so vocally and vehemently judgmental? Where's the love you called us to live out? Do they believe the things they say honor or defend you?

Great questions. Let's chat with God.

God, Can We Chat?

Consider the Facts

What specific incident(s) has caused you to ask this question? (Just the facts, ma'am!)

- Are you thinking about a specific person or group of people? If so, who?

- What specific comments about you, God, or the others have been difficult or hurtful?

Honor the Story You're Telling Yourself

Get curious about your emotions and inner narrative around this question. In the following exercises, use this prompt: *The story I'm telling myself is . . .*

- When you think about Christians who have said hurtful things, how do you feel about them, yourself, God, and the church?

- Do you feel their words carry a hidden message to you and/or others? If so, what is it?

- If you haven't put words to these feelings and inner narrative before, how has naming them been helpful or enlightening?

Ask God What He Has to Say

Prayerfully ask God to show you how he sees things, including you, and what he might want to say to you as a friend today.

- Imagine God beside you in the very moment you hear these hurtful things. What's he doing or saying?

- If you and Jesus met for coffee today, what might he say about these people, their comments, and the aftermath?

- Intellectually, you might know God loves Christians who say hurtful things, but if you struggle on a heart level to see anything lovable about them, ask God to help you see them as he does.

Team Up with God Moving Forward

As you walk through daily life and face its inevitable frustrations, questions, and doubts, how can you intentionally link arms with God and doubt-walk through your unanswered questions?

- Even if these messages and hurtful words don't stop, how might you be able to walk with God in compassion and love for others and yourself? If taking that path feels too hard, ask God to help you.

- In what way might God be asking you to love him and his Christ, even if you don't love his Christians?

- What boundaries, if any, might you need in order to protect yourself from future harm?

Lord, I pray in the words of Saint Francis:
Make me an instrument of your peace.
Where there is hatred, let me sow love;
where there is injury, pardon.
Where there are jerks, Lord, let me sow tolerance.
And PS, when I'm the jerk, please let me know.
Amen.

Chat Notes

God, who's right and who's wrong on this?

Lord, you saw this conversation play out time and time again whenever someone asked a specific theological question. This week was no different: "So, what's your view on predestination and infant baptism?"

Scanning the circle of chairs around me, I saw a few heads nodding, one eyebrow raised, and everyone looking expectantly at Al as they munched on deli-made sandwiches and kettle chips. This was a welcome lunch, CityChurch style. It was a chance for any new folks to get to know us, hear more about who we were as a church, and meet the staff. Eventually—and often just as we were about to wrap up—someone would drop a doozy of a question they'd been desperate to ask, but this guy obviously couldn't contain himself. Understandably, if people were going to make this their church home, they wanted to know if our beliefs aligned with theirs and where we stood on one theological issue or another. I got it.

The month before, it had been questions about creation and women in leadership. The month before that, homosexuality and transubstantiation. The month before that had been a fun jaunt into the continuation or cessation of spiritual gifts, as well as whether we were premillennial, postmillennial, or amillennial in our interpretation of the end times and Christ's second coming.

You name it, we've been asked about it. It's important but also exhausting.

Thankfully, Al was prepared, his notepad ready. He began in the same deliberate way, slowly drawing a big circle in the center of the page, making sure everyone could see what he was doing.

"The thing is," he explained with an understanding smile, "these issues are important, and we do have views on all of them, which I'm more than happy to talk about. But before I do, I want to share what is first and foremost and central to who we are as a church. And it's especially important when there are numerous hot topics like these and even more opinions on each one. When we focus on the issues, we begin to draw a line, a demarcation of where we stand."

Retracing the outline of the circle, he continued, "We plant a flag saying 'This side is with us, that side isn't.' Unfortunately, over time, what happens is we all end up focusing on the line and who's in or out. For us or against us."

He smiled, beginning to draw an embarrassingly bad stick figure in the middle of the circle, then went on. "At CityChurch, we try and focus *first* on the person of Jesus and continually moving towards him rather than focusing on the lines." Drawing large black arrows pointing at the stick-figure Jesus, he said, "That way our eyes are fixed on him, not the line. In some areas of your faith, you might be closer to Jesus than other people; in others, you may be struggling and further away. But we're all moving towards Jesus and trying, with his help, to become more like him, together. It's with that in mind that we're able to discuss these other important topics."

Lord, I'm proud of how Al and I have always handled this in ministry. But it sure would have made things easier if we all knew what's "right." Surely you have an opinion on these topics, so why didn't you make it clearer?

With forty-five thousand denominations worldwide and two hundred in the US alone,[7] it's no wonder we get our faith knickers in a twist when it comes to trying to figure out what to believe and who's right and who's wacko. So often we proclaim the sentiment that has been attributed to everyone from Saint Augustine to John Wesley to the Moravians: "In essentials, unity; in nonessentials, liberty; in all things, love." That is, until we're asked to decide what our "essentials" and "nonessentials" are exactly. Some topics are abundantly clear—for example, snake handling? Probably not even a nonessential. But other topics, such as the debate over evolution and creation, may be a core essential for some people while for others it's a peripheral nonessential.

So what are we to do when we're caught in the crossfire? Like deer in the headlights of numerous competing opinions, each urging us to figure it out, take a side, know what we think, and, whatever we do, not cross the line clearly laid out by our friends, family, and church, we question ourselves, our beliefs, our church.

We're left asking, *What should I believe, God? Who's right and who's wrong? The church down the road is full of great people, but their stance on this one issue feels wonky. How do I know what's correct?*

Great questions. Let's chat with God.

God, Can We Chat?

Consider the Facts

What specific incident(s) has caused you to ask this question? (Just the facts, ma'am!)

- Is there a particular theological issue you've been thinking about that's driving this question?

- What specific messages have you picked up around the need to have clarity on certain issues?

- If you've ever felt on the "wrong" side of a theological issue, what were the circumstances that led to your feeling this way?

Honor the Story You're Telling Yourself

Get curious about your emotions and inner narrative around this question. In the following exercises, use this prompt: *The story I'm telling myself is . . .*

- What's your biggest fear when it comes to where you stand or where you are feeling pulled to on some of the more divisive issues?

- How would your feelings towards yourself change if your views shifted?

- Complete some of these sentences:

  - If I change my views on *X*, then *Y* will happen.

  - I need to be clear about what I believe because . . .

  - Those with different views are . . .

Ask God What He Has to Say

Prayerfully ask God to show you how he sees things, including you, and what he might want to say to you as a friend today.

- Does it matter what I believe about this particular issue?

- My views on some things are shifting, and in a lot of areas I have no clue where to land. Is that okay? Will you still love me?

- Help me love myself and others as our views differ and shift.

Team Up with God Moving Forward

As you walk through daily life and face its inevitable frustrations, questions, and doubts, how can you intentionally link arms with God and doubt-walk through your unanswered questions?

- The next time you come across an issue you're unsure about, ask God for his grace and to help you fix your eyes on him as you figure things out together.

- In what ways can you love yourself and others better as you wrestle with divisive issues, even when you have differing views?

- What would offering yourself grace in this season look like?

God of us all,
whose love knows no bounds,
keep my eyes fixed on you,
"the way and the truth and the life" (John 14:6).
In our theological debates and wanderings
may I offer others, as well as myself,
the grace you first gave me.
Guide us in all truth.
Unite us as one church
as we try to live out and "proclaim
the mystery of Christ" (Col. 4:3).
Amen.

Chat Notes

■ God, are you good? This doesn't feel good.

Lord, Al's sitting crumpled on the floor weeping, trembling, his head buried in his hands. It isn't that he doesn't want to go on; it's that he simply can't. His body's shutting down, refusing to press on.

For the consummate English gentleman you know he is, raised to keep it all together, do his duty, not complain, and stand firm in the face of adversity, it feels like the end of himself. In his eyes, he's a failure.

Seeing him going through this is awful. You're supposed to be good. I've always believed you are. But this? It doesn't feel good at all.

~

Al's was a breakdown brought on by years of hard work, pushing his limits, staying the course when others would have run for the door, and a deep desire to do everything God had called him to. Layer on top of that years of painful church planting struggles, followed by holding the family together during my cancer diagnosis, and then navigating the church through the chaos of the pandemic, and he'd hit a wall.

It wasn't pretty. Exhaustion, depression, insomnia, and the (in his eyes) mortifying need to step down from ministry for a season, all sealed the deal on his perceived failings.

There are T-shirts, mugs, caps, sweatshirts, and even cozies and dog collars (of the canine, not clerical, variety) emblazoned with the phrase "Life is good." But the truth is, it's often not. It's an uplifting mantra, spurring us to live life fully. But if we take it literally, when we're hit by one of life's curveballs, we're left wondering, *Is it though?*

Life is full of devastating breakdowns and diseases that rob us of our dignity as well as our remaining years. It's crammed with grief at the loss of people we cherish, and it's teeming with wars and disasters on a global scale.

Life might be good in a silver-lining kind of way, but a lot of the time it can feel really, really bad.

When we discover our teen's been cutting, or witness a hurricane flatten our neighborhood, or sit surrounded by bills and wonder how to pay the mortgage, or stop our scroll as another war starts and innocent people die by the thousands, we question whether God can see it too. And if he can and doesn't intervene, we wonder how he can be good after all. Because this sure doesn't look or feel good.

We shake our heads and demand, "God, how can you be good when this all feels so wrong? Surely if you were good—*really* good—you'd stop it, change it, fix it, do something? Where is your mercy and justice? If it's there, show us. Tell us, God, are you good? Because from where we're sitting it sure doesn't look like it."

Great questions. Let's chat with God.

God, Can We Chat?

Consider the Facts

What specific incident(s) has caused you to ask this question? (Just the facts, ma'am!)

- What's brought you to the conclusion that God might not be as good as you once thought?

- Have you always worried about this, or has something changed?

- If something has changed, name it. Be specific, listing as many facts as you can.

Honor the Story You're Telling Yourself

Get curious about your emotions and inner narrative around this question. In the following exercises, use this prompt: *The story I'm telling myself is . . .*

- Think about this question and what's led you to ask it, and brain dump every emotion, thought, and feeling it brings to the surface.

- What pattern or story about you and God is emerging?

- Is it one you've heard before? If so, from whom and when?

Ask God What He Has to Say

Prayerfully ask God to show you how he sees things, including you, and what he might want to say to you as a friend today.

- If you're going through some hard things right now, take a moment to ask God where he is in them. What images, Scriptures, or words come to mind as you do?

- If God wrote you an encouraging card to help you get through this difficult time, what would it say?

- How is God encouraging you through other people?

Team Up with God Moving Forward

As you walk through daily life and face its inevitable frustrations, questions, and doubts, how can you intentionally link arms with God and doubt-walk through your unanswered questions?

- What do you need to do to begin walking with God in this mystery, trusting that his goodness outweighs the bad you're seeing?

- Take a short walk, and as you go, take time to notice or think of three things that remind you of God's goodness.

- As you move forward, is there a belief, assumption, person, place, or thing God might be asking you to hold on to or let go of?

A Blessing for When Life's Far from Good

For the ones who wonder whether God is good,
or if his goodness comes and goes
or skips us entirely,
abandoning us to our fear.
In our grief and pain, questions and lament,
may we taste and see God's goodness
even as we doubt it.
May we carry our doubts to him in open-eyed wonder,
trusting his goodness goes before us.

Chat Notes

God, do you even care?

Lord, Julie's smiling up at me from her Christmas card as she does every year, her eyes twinkling mischievously like they did in college—but she's in a motorized wheelchair. When did that happen? When did her autoimmune disease trap her there? I know it's June, and I've only just grabbed the post mailed to our old address. I know I could have kept up with her better. I know I could have prayed for her more. I KNOW! But Lord, what have you let happen?

Julie was my best buddy from university. While I, a zoology major, enjoyed subjects like animal behavior, Julie, a medic, wrestled long into the night with advanced anatomy and physiology, biochemistry, microbiology, and pathology so she could do what she loved most—be fully focused on others.

As a doctor, she'd risen through the ranks to consultant anesthetist, professor, and then respected author, before teaching the professors themselves and working with hospitals and surgeons to reduce surgical errors and mortality rates. A life of service, helping others in need.

Her Christmas card tells another, more devastating story. An incurable autoimmune disease has left her wheelchair-bound and robbed her of her job, playing with her kids, swimming in the sea, and nights out with friends. After a life spent helping others, she needs help to get up the stairs and put on her shoes. Eventually she'll need someone to feed her.

The unfairness unravels me as her indomitable grin lights up her card, almost eclipsing the wheelchair she sits in.

Intellectually, we know bad stuff happens to good people (and vice versa) and the world is broken. We know, as Edward Abbey reminds us in *The Fool's Progress*, "Life is unfair and it's not fair that life is unfair."[8] We might even have asked why God allows pain, heartache, and suffering, but it's not until the pain stares back at us from a Christmas card, wakes us with a 3 a.m. call, or spits its venom over the internet that the question tightens its grip, cutting off our faith's oxygen.

When it's our body breaking down, our kid who's taken an overdose after being bullied online, or our neighborhood school mourning the senseless loss of bright young futures after another shooter's gone wild, the question shifts. When our hearts break over the swollen bellies of babies starving amidst the ravages of war or young girls sold as sex slaves when they should be riding their bikes, our questions change.

We no longer simply wonder (intellectually or theologically), *Why does God allow suffering?* We emotionally shake our heads in disbelief and challenge God directly: *Why are you allowing this, God? Don't you care?*

Our belief that God cares deeply for everyone and about everything is as robust as wet tissue paper, threatening to disintegrate with our next tear-stained prayer. *Don't you hear us, see us, care about us, God? How can you if you're letting this happen?*

Great questions. Let's chat with God.

God, Can We Chat?

Consider the Facts

What specific incident(s) has caused you to ask this question? (Just the facts, ma'am!)

- When was the first time this question became personal?

- What had happened to make your questioning shift from merely intellectual or theological to emotional and personal?

- Who is your heart breaking for—yourself, someone else, or both?

Honor the Story You're Telling Yourself

Get curious about your emotions and inner narrative around this question. In the following exercises, use this prompt: *The story I'm telling myself is . . .*

- Imagine telling the story of what's happened to someone who hasn't heard about it. Describe the injustice, anger, disbelief, or any other emotion you feel.

- What's the story about God you're hearing as you tell the story?

- What's the narrative you're telling yourself about who you and/or the people suffering this injustice are to God?

Ask God What He Has to Say

Prayerfully ask God to show you how he sees things, including you, and what he might want to say to you as a friend today.

- Pause a moment to close your eyes, take a deep breath in and out, and imagine Jesus sitting with you in this painful situation. What's he doing, saying, or showing you?

- As you sit with him, what images, Scriptures, or words come to mind?

- Now imagine Jesus giving you a gift to unwrap. What is it and what does it say to you?

Team Up with God Moving Forward

As you walk through daily life and face its inevitable frustrations, questions, and doubts, how can you intentionally link arms with God and doubt-walk through your unanswered questions?

- If God cares desperately, despite all your heartache, what might he be asking you to do slap bang in the middle of this frustrating paradox to believe that?

- How might God be asking you to partner with him to address this injustice or care for the person who's hurting, even if that's you?

- When your heartache's unbearable or your questions scream louder than normal, what small thing can you do to lean on God, even if everything in you wants to ignore him?

As my head and heart bicker over whether you care,
may I be the kind of doubting believer
who reaches for you anyway,
because, at the end of the day,
I think you do care.
Please don't prove me wrong.
Amen.

Chat Notes

■ God, why can't I stop worrying?

My eyes. They're so heavy. Refusing to open. It's dark. The hospital's humming its nighttime melody, pulling me back under. Bit by bit, my eyes adjust to the soft fluorescent light as I drag myself out of my morphine-induced sleep. *Urghh, what's this? I'm lying in something warm and sticky. Oh @#$%&! . . . is that blood? Surely it's not mine. Where on earth is it coming from?*

⁓

You don't need to be a doctor to know lying in a pool of blood—yours or anyone else's—isn't good. Yanking the emergency cord, I summoned a nurse before panic-praying.

Had the surgery to remove the tumor (from the orifice I don't care to mention in polite company) gone wrong? Was I bleeding out?*

In that heart-stopping moment, I wanted to trust God, feel his peace, and stop worrying. I tried—honestly I did. I just couldn't. The worry wheels spinning out of control in my brain Simply. Wouldn't. Stop. I didn't need to sort of trust him. I needed to really, *really* trust him.

The platitude "faith over fear" has been absorbed into the fabric of our faith, but it paints faith as a magic eraser. *Wipe away fear with our new and improved worry-erasing sponge filled with fast-acting faith. Never let worry hold you back again! Brought to you by your trusty Bible verse 1 John 4:18.*

It suggests if we had enough faith, we'd be able to sleep peacefully and hope would have a fair shot at rising. We'd laugh again and thrive instead of barely surviving life, even if

---

*PS: If you're wondering if I was okay, thank you! It *was* my blood, but it was some sort of normal postsurgical draining no one warned me was a possibility. I was (and am) all good.

173

our cancer's progressing or we're struggling to pay our rent. If we just had enough faith, worry wouldn't have a hold on us or have a chance to derail our faith.

The truth is, we don't think about trusting God until we really need to. Until crisis hits. Then, with every ounce of faith, gumption, and fear-fueled strength as well as some calming breath prayers, we hang on to God for dear life—but still the worry lingers. These are all helpful things to do, but worry is rarely silenced or slain once and for all.

Maybe you're fresh from waking up in your own pool of blood. Perhaps you've recently experienced heartbreaking loss, grief, and pain. Or maybe you're not just anxious now and then but your life is ruled by persistent, debilitating worry that interferes with daily activities, leaving you restless, on edge, easily fatigued, unable to concentrate, or struggling to sleep.[9]

No matter what brings us here, we're left asking, *Why can't I stop worrying, God? I trust you (Prov. 3:5), and I try not to worry (Matt. 6:25) or be anxious about anything (Phil. 4:6), but I can't help it. Is worry a sin if you told us not to worry? What's the deal? Am I doing something wrong? Is it even worth trusting you?*

Great questions. Let's chat with God.

God, Can We Chat?

Before we chat with God, I'd be a bad friend if I didn't remind you that I'm not a therapist, counselor, or doctor. If you need to seek help from a professional, please do. It's not a sign of weakness in you or your relationship with God. There are times when the best way to love ourselves is to get the professional help we need to deal with our worries and anxiety alongside our faith.

Consider the Facts

What specific incident(s) has caused you to ask this question? (Just the facts, ma'am!)

- Are you worried about one particular thing, or a load of things stacked on top of each other?

- Does your worry come and go, or are you in a constant state of worry?

- When it comes to worry and your faith, what specific messages have you been told?

- What would you need to happen, know, believe, or be reassured of in order for you to not worry?

Honor the Story You're Telling Yourself

Get curious about your emotions and inner narrative around this question. In the following exercises, use this prompt: *The story I'm telling myself is . . .*

- What is a core belief underpinning and fueling your worry? Examples: "I can't make a mistake." "Things never work out for me." "Bad things always happen to me."

- What do you believe your worry says about you in general as a person?

- What do you believe about the thread connecting worry to your faith and God?

Ask God What He Has to Say

Prayerfully ask God to show you how he sees things, including you, and what he might want to say to you as a friend today.

- Imagine telling God that core belief you named. What do you think he would say in response? Does he agree? What alternative mantra might he offer you?

- In Matthew 6:34, Jesus says, "Therefore do not worry about tomorrow, for tomorrow will worry about itself. Each day has enough trouble of its own." How might God be asking you to see this verse as a gift, not a goal?

Team Up with God Moving Forward

As you walk through daily life and face its inevitable frustrations, questions, and doubts, how can you intentionally link arms with God and doubt-walk through your unanswered questions?

- Reread Matthew 6:34. How might God be asking you to team up with him to only solve what is solvable *today*?

- Imagine sitting with Jesus and handing him a box full of your unsolvable worries. What does he do with it? How might you carry it together?

- When you next tell yourself the story behind your care or worry or core belief, ask Jesus to help you replace it with the mantra he gave you.

Lord, I'm more of a worry wart than either of us would like.
My mind spins like a Vitamix blender
with no Off button,
no plug to pull.
It won't stop.
I trust you—I do—but still it spins.
And it's exhausting.
Share my load.
Take my fears.
Carry me.
And calm my strobing heart.
Amen.

Chat Notes

_____

_____

_____

_____

_____

_____

_____

_____

▪ God, I don't get it.

If you asked me face-to-face, God, whether I really expected to "get it" when it comes to all things GodFaithChurch, I'd chuckle, even let out one of those ugly snort-laughs I can't control, shake my head, and sheepishly admit, "Of course not."

Deep down I know and accept a level of mystery and unknowability in my faith and relationship with you, and I'm willing to go with it. Yet so often "I don't get it, God!" erupts from my mouth the millisecond the poop hits the fan and lands in my inbox, or when the church, the Bible, or your followers don't make any God-given logical sense.

So I'll say it straight now, God: I don't get it.

———

A popular high school athlete takes his life on a sunny Wednesday afternoon. A militant group quotes Scripture as they ostracize those in need of love. A warlord murders Christians hiding in the sanctuary of a church.

What do you do when you discover your daughter's been taking laxatives to get a thigh gap and your friend's husband has been abusive? Or when church feels hard and you're not sure whether to stay or go? Or when you're still trying to forgive your mum for leaving when you were six?

We know in our heads how ungettable God is and how, if that ever changed, either we'd have risen to his level or he'd be lowered to ours—and we both know what a disaster both options would be on so many levels. Yet our heads and our hearts still cry, "I don't get it, God."

Socrates is famous for reminding us that the only true wisdom is in knowing you know nothing. And when it comes to knowing God's ways, Paul seems to agree. As the early church debated the issue of eating food that had been offered to idols, he argued, "Anyone who claims to know all the answers doesn't really know very much" (1 Cor. 8:2 NLT). But living in this place of not knowing is humbling, uncomfortable, and often heart-wrenching.

Answers tidy our stories up neatly. They close wounds, shut doors, open windows, and let the fresh air in. Certainty puts solid ground under our sinking feet and pulls air into our gasping lungs. Knowledge and certainty feel powerful and comforting, and they fuel our will to go on.

So what are we meant to do when, despite knowing how futile it is, we still want to sit God down and ask what the deal is? Every bone in our broken bodies, every corner of our aching hearts, every neuron in our confused little brains longs for God to spill the beans and help us get it.

No matter what's brought you to this place, "God, I don't get it" is a great question. So let's chat with him.

God, Can We Chat?

Consider the Facts

What specific incident(s) has caused you to ask this question? (Just the facts, ma'am!)

- For you, is "God, I don't get it" a genuine question looking for answers or more of a resigned lament of how things are?

- Are you normally someone who has the answers and is the voice of reason and perspective?

- Have you always struggled with this question or is it new? If you've just started to say this to God, what in particular precipitated it?

Honor the Story You're Telling Yourself

Get curious about your emotions and inner narrative around this question. In the following exercises, use this prompt: *The story I'm telling myself is . . .*

- How does having answers to your questions normally make you feel? Conversely, how does being unable to explain things make you feel?

- If you never "get it" with the issues you'd like clarity from God on, what do you imagine will happen?

- How does this issue affect your relationship with God?

Ask God What He Has to Say

Prayerfully ask God to show you how he sees things, including you, and what he might want to say to you as a friend today.

- Imagine yourself on a walk with God where he asks what's on your mind. When you tell him you don't get it, how does he respond?

- What's the one thing you think God wants you to know in this place of uncertainty?

- What Scripture verses or stories come to mind when you and God chat? Take a moment to reread them and pray back to God what comes to mind.

Team Up with God Moving Forward

As you walk through daily life and face its inevitable frustrations, questions, and doubts, how can you intentionally link arms with God and doubt-walk through your unanswered questions?

- What do you need in order to keep walking with God even if you never "get it"?

- Whatever it is you need, turn it into a prayer and ask God to provide it in lieu of answering your question.

In my need to get it, Lord, love me anyway.
In my longing to figure it out, tether me to who you are.
And in my discomfort at the not knowing,
may I learn to humbly embrace how little I'm sure of,
taking comfort in the reality that
until I accept that you alone know it all,
it will never be enough.
Thankfully, Lord, despite my best attempts,
I'm not God. You are.
Let's keep it that way!
Amen.

Chat Notes

▪ God, why did this happen?

Lord, whenever I find myself asking this question, two things are usually true. Firstly, what's happened is far from wonderful, because if something brilliant happens, I might thank you briefly, but I confess I rarely ask why I've had the good fortune to experience it.

Secondly, and more importantly, while a fraction of me does want to know the reason, what I'm more worried about is whether what I believe to be true about you—that you're the perfect force for good in the movie of life—is, in fact, true. Because what's happened makes me doubt it. What if I'm wrong, Lord?

~

Like C. S. Lewis, my worry isn't so much about discovering I don't believe in God, but that I believe awful things about him.[10] A pit forms in my stomach when I imagine he's not who I thought he was.

If you're anything like me, your fear behind this question is the suspicion that maybe God's not the good guy you've always believed. For most of us, this would be soul-destroying and more than our faith could withstand. So we ask God why in the hopes of hearing something to ease our fears.

Many of us crave the certainty of knowing we haven't wasted our time, or given our hearts to a swindler or a dupe, or simply been wrong all along. Just thinking about this tightens my chest, knots my insides, and weighs me down like a sinking stone.

Whether you really do want to know the ins and outs of why something happened or you're nursing a deeper, unvoiced fear of God not being who you've always believed him to be, the questions remain the same:

Why did this happen, God? What were you thinking? Were you thinking about me/us/them? What does this mean or say about who you are?

Great questions. Let's chat with God.

God, Can We Chat?

Consider the Facts

What specific incident(s) has caused you to ask this question? (Just the facts, ma'am!)

- Give yourself some time to think or write about what happened that led to your asking this question. Was it one specific event or a series of events? Who or what was hurt, damaged, lost, or broken?

- What ripples has this event sent through your life and family?

- Name what is worse for you now than before it happened.

Honor the Story You're Telling Yourself

Get curious about your emotions and inner narrative around this question. In the following exercises, use this prompt: *The story I'm telling myself is . . .*

- Who are you since this happened? How did it change you?

- How has this hard thing changed how you see yourself?

- What do you now believe must be true of you? Of God? Of your relationship with God?

Ask God What He Has to Say

Prayerfully ask God to show you how he sees things, including you, and what he might want to say to you as a friend today.

- Prayerfully ask God to help you imagine the scene as the terrible thing that happened plays in front of you like a movie. Where is God? What is he doing and saying? Who is he with?

- What specific questions do you want to ask God about this? Do you feel that you can ask him?

- What might God want you to know or understand today?

Team Up with God Moving Forward

As you walk through daily life and face its inevitable frustrations, questions, and doubts, how can you intentionally link arms with God and doubt-walk through your unanswered questions?

- How might you share the burden of the grief, loss, hurt, or worry with God?

- What might believing God is good, even when things like this happen, look like for you on a daily basis?

- What might it look like to be willing to invite God into the good, bad, and ugly parts of your life, even if you never have this question answered fully?

A Blessing in Our Whys

*May we who secretly fear God's not the good guy after all
or wonder what on earth he's thinking
face our fears in his presence.
May we grapple with his unknowable wisdom
and the ungettable vastness of his love,
and together may we find a way to keep
believing in his goodness,
come what may.*

Chat Notes

■ God, how do I trust you?

The kids' trust jars live on our kitchen counter next to the toaster. Lord, you've seen the empty jam jars fill with colored water, empty, then fill again, as they earn our trust, lose it, and win it back in a never-ending cycle of teachable moments. You've heard us explain, "Trust is both given and earned. You become trustworthy by earning what we've already given you—like following through on a responsibility, walking the dog, or being home by curfew. Or you can lose it by going behind our backs, lying, or failing to keep your word. It's how trust in real life works." You've seen how the kids think it's a game—until their jars run dangerously low, that is—but it's our way of helping them see that trust might not be free but it can be grown.

Except trust doesn't work this way with you, God, does it?

God is God, after all. He shouldn't need to earn our trust or prove his goodness. But still, I apply this "trust jar" logic to our relationship on a daily basis, assuming he's failed in some trust-destroying move the moment he doesn't come through on something I think he should have done.

It's a bold and warped role reversal where I'm the one setting the standard for what's acceptable, trustworthy, and true to his word—but who am I to say? Who do I think I am to arbitrate what God *should* do and whether he's kept his promises? No one, that's who!

So how do we learn to trust God when the goal posts seem to constantly move? If we go by our own standards, he appears to be good, fair, and easy to trust one moment, and the next minute he seems petulant, fickle, distant, and like the last person we want to rely on.

I've written more than my fair share of words on how we can learn to trust God when life falls apart and how trusting God doesn't just happen the moment we meet Jesus but is a choice we have to make daily. (I've even created a five-step plan to help us do that.) But I'm still left asking, "How do I trust you, God?" more often than I care to admit.

When God doesn't work by *our* rules or meet *our* expectations, and our logical brains don't understand his ways (or apparent lack of them), we're left asking over and over, *How do I trust you, God? Are you trustworthy? Because I want to rely on you but I'm nervous to let go. What does trusting you look like when my world's been swept away?*

Great questions. Let's chat with God.

God, Can We Chat?

Consider the Facts

What specific incident(s) has caused you to ask this question? (Just the facts, ma'am!)

- Name an area of your life where you're struggling to trust God.

- Have you always found it hard to entrust this person, place, or thing to God, or is this new?

- What happened to shift your belief about how trust-worthy God is?

Honor the Story You're Telling Yourself

Get curious about your emotions and inner narrative around this question. In the following exercises, use this prompt: *The story I'm telling myself is . . .*

- When you struggle to trust God, what does this struggle say about you or the strength of your faith?

- When you think about wanting to trust God but not being able to, how do you feel about yourself? Specifically name your own emotions.

Ask God What He Has to Say

Prayerfully ask God to show you how he sees things, including you, and what he might want to say to you as a friend today.

- Take a moment to imagine God sitting with you on a park bench, and tell him how you want to trust him but can't. How do you feel before you tell him? What does he do or say? What do you know to be true afterwards?

- Ask God if there's anyone or anything you're relying on more than him.

Team Up with God Moving Forward

As you walk through daily life and face its inevitable frustrations, questions, and doubts, how can you intentionally link arms with God and doubt-walk through your unanswered questions?

- What might trusting God in small, manageable bites look like for you? Be as specific and practical as you can.

- Ask God to help you trust him more and to show you tangible ways he's trustworthy that you might have missed.

- Create a trust jar for God and add a little bit more colored water each time you see God show up in your life. As your trust jar fills, you'll not only have a visible record of his trustworthiness to reflect on when it becomes hard again, but you'll also have a jar full of his trustworthiness to thank him for.

I confess, Lord,
trusting you with all my heart is hard.
Leaning not on my own understanding is harder still.
Forgive me.
When wounds declare your untrustworthiness,
help me hear otherwise.
May your trust jar always overflow,
reminding me it's safe to trust you
even when every bone in my body screams, "Don't!"
Come, Lord.
I trust; help my lack of trust.
Amen.

Chat Notes

God, I'm doing all the right things; why haven't you fixed it?

There it is in grainy black and white—my little broad bean. But it's quiet, motionless. No beating heart or sign of life on the ultrasound monitor to tell us it's okay. This little life has ended mere weeks after it valiantly began, and I love its gusto and willingness to try. Another loss, Lord. Another unanswered prayer.

It wasn't our first miscarriage, and wouldn't be our last. But despite already having what many consider the perfect family—a boy and a girl, one for each hand, one for each knee, one for each parent to hoist onto their shoulders—we were sure our family wasn't complete yet. Al and I had each been raised in the chaos of a family of five, with the constant squabbles of who sits in the middle and the perpetual fight for attention, and we were pretty sure God wasn't telling us to do otherwise.

With friends struggling to get pregnant, I knew how fortunate we were to have any kids, let alone two rambunctious little mites. But we weren't ready to give up. So we prayed and prayed, had friends pray for us and with us, laid hold of God's promises—then fasted and prayed some more.

As we waded through miscarriage after miscarriage, some friends were also trying for baby number three. Like us, they already had two kids, but unlike us, both were girls. They were now desperate for a boy and were utterly convinced their weird food regimen, his new tight undies, and only trying at certain times of the month would get them their longed-for boy.

A few months later they shared their happy news—they were expecting and it was a boy!

A few days after that, we miscarried. Again.

190

What were we doing wrong? What had they done right? Why hadn't God fixed it?

Maybe, like me, you have a secret suspicion that prayer is hackable and life is fixable when we partner with God in just the right way. That if we pray the right prayers, are aligned with his will, have enough belief to fuel a revival, repeat God's promises back to him, fast, and close with a rousing "in the name of Jesus," we'll crack the code and win the jackpot.

Of course, we know God doesn't work this way, but the disappointed, waiting, longing part of us secretly clings to the hope he does. Then, when the formula fails, we're left telling God how we did all the right things and everything he asked of us, and wondering what went wrong?

Didn't you hear me, God? Was my faith not strong enough? Are you mad at me? Ignoring me? Or do you have favorites? Do I need to repent of something? (And if so, please tell me, because I have no idea what I've done.) Do I need to forgive someone or fast a little longer? I haven't a clue what you want from me. Why haven't you fixed this?

Great questions. Let's chat with God.

God, Can We Chat?

Consider the Facts

What specific incident(s) has caused you to ask this question? (Just the facts, ma'am!)

- Describe the diagnosis, conflict, addiction, financial worry, or difficult situation God hasn't fixed for you.

- Name the things you've been doing in the hopes God would fix it.

- How do you want God to sort it out?

Honor the Story You're Telling Yourself

Get curious about your emotions and inner narrative around this question. In the following exercises, use this prompt: *The story I'm telling myself is . . .*

- What messages have you picked up in life that tell you if you behave a certain way, measure up to the right standards, or check all the boxes, God will come through for you?

- Why do you think God hasn't intervened to fix things?

- If God never fixes it, what do you think that might say about you or him? What about when he seems to answer other people's prayers but not yours?

Ask God What He Has to Say

Prayerfully ask God to show you how he sees things, including you, and what he might want to say to you as a friend today.

- Write the things God hasn't fixed on scraps of paper. Now put them all in an old shoebox or packing box and close the lid. As you do, tell Jesus exactly how you feel about both the box and him, given he appears to have passively stood by. Thinking of this as a psalm of lament gives us the freedom to be fully honest with him.

- In your mind's eye, what does Jesus do with the box? What might he be saying to you about what's in the box?

- Is there something Jesus wants you to know about you?

Team Up with God Moving Forward

As you walk through daily life and face its inevitable frustrations, questions, and doubts, how can you intentionally link arms with God and doubt-walk through your unanswered questions?

- How might God be asking you to stop trying so hard to do all the right things and simply be with him?

- Take the box and put it somewhere that symbolizes your leaving it in God's care—maybe at the foot of a cross, on your Bible, even in the trash bin. Before walking away, ask him to look after it for you.

> *Knees calloused, days fasted, Scriptures read.*
> *Faith roused, forgiveness given, repentance offered.*
> *What more can I do?*
> *You're God, the Provider and Healer,*
> *who seems to step up for others but not for me.*
> *Why, Lord? Why?*
> *Through all that's*
> *unfixable and un-figure-out-able,*
> *walk with me, hold me, strengthen me with hope.*
> *When I'm bitter and jealous of those*
> *whose prayers you answer,*
> *forgive me.*
> *Teach me how to love you as well as them*
> *and even myself.*
> *Your will and not mine be done . . . I guess.*
> *Amen.*

Chat Notes

_____

_____

_____

_____

_____

_____

_____

_____

_____

_____

_____

_____

_____

_____

_____

God, is the Bible really *your* Word?

Shhh, come here and listen in. Be careful, don't make a sound. They mustn't know we're eavesdropping. Amy, Jason, and Joan are fiercely debating whether the Bible is God's Word, and their opinions couldn't be more different.*

Amy: The Bible is literal, infallible, inerrant, and our authority on everything. How do I know? Well, God's perfect and he wrote a book that's flawless (Prov. 30:5), perfect (Ps. 19:7), pure (Ps. 12:6), and God-breathed (2 Tim. 3:16). There isn't a mistake within its pages, and we must take it literally.

Jason: How can you say that? My local library is a collection of books written by different authors at different times for different purposes, all brought together in one place. I don't believe in my local library or call it the inspired Word of God, so why should I do the same for the Bible—which is, for all intents and purposes, the same thing. And don't try using the Bible to justify the Bible. It's a circular argument, like saying, "If I say I'm an elf, then I must be an elf."

Joan: You're both off base. Sure, the Bible's inspired by God, and I'm sure he guided the hands of those who wrote it. But it's not inerrant if what you mean by that is "error free." It's our inspired, sacred, and authoritative text, but it was written and then translated many times over by humans, so it's not infallible. But you definitely can't read the Bible and not see God's handiwork woven through it.

~

*This is an imaginary conversation, but it's based on what could have been a real conversation between a few of the people who've come through our church doors but never, as far as we know, shared their views with each other.

As leaders of a nondenominational church, we heard it all when it comes to the Bible.

Recent research tells us half of all Americans (not just Christian Americans) view the Bible as inspired by God but don't take everything in it literally. One in five Americans do take everything in the Bible literally, while almost one-third of Americans see it quite literally as a library.[11]

No matter how you view the Bible, the chances are that at some point you've questioned not just what's printed in its pages but how inspired, inerrant, infallible, or authoritative it is.

So what are we meant to do when we struggle to know whether the Bible is simply a pocket-sized library of poems, fictional stories, and helpful yet sometimes odd teachings, or something much more—God's true Word? Do we hold it lightly, then cherry-pick the easily digestible parts that make sense in the twenty-first century while casually ditching the rest?

Are we guilty, as Gandhi purportedly accused, of holding a document containing enough dynamite to utterly transform our lives, turn the world upside down, and bring peace to a battle-torn planet but treating it as though it is nothing more than a piece of literature? Should we double down and hold firm, unswayed? Is there another way to navigate this complex and much-debated book?

Just tell us, God, is it your Word or not? Have we turned it into something it's not, in one way or another?

Great questions. Let's chat with God.

God, Can We Chat?

Consider the Facts

What specific incident(s) has caused you to ask this question? (Just the facts, ma'am!)

- What beliefs or messages about the Bible did you receive growing up?

- What, if anything, has made you reevaluate your thinking?

- Why are you asking this particular question at this time?

Honor the Story You're Telling Yourself

Get curious about your emotions and inner narrative around this question. In the following exercises, use this prompt: *The story I'm telling myself is . . .*

- How do you feel about the idea that God has approved every word in the Bible?

- What might be true about you or God if the Bible is his inspired Word?

- How might your view of God change if the Bible is not inerrant or if not all the stories it contains are literal?

- If the Bible is not just *about* God but *from* God, what does this say about you when you struggle with it or it doesn't make sense?

Ask God What He Has to Say

Prayerfully ask God to show you how he sees things, including you, and what he might want to say to you as a friend today.

- Prayerfully ask God why he gave us the Bible and what he hopes you receive from it.

- Take a moment to ask God to show you how he feels about the Bible, asking him to bring specific Scripture verses and stories to mind.

- As you chat with God, ask him to show you if how you view the Bible changes how he views you.

Team Up with God Moving Forward

As you walk through daily life and face its inevitable frustrations, questions, and doubts, how can you intentionally link arms with God and doubt-walk through your unanswered questions?

- Take a moment to ask God to help you love him and the Bible, even in this place of uncertainty.

- Write down some of the questions you're carrying about the Bible. Pray them back to God without demanding answers but simply to share them with him, then tuck them into your Bible as a way of entrusting them to God.

> *Lord, your Word is a lamp to my feet,*
> *but is it your Word?*
> *In my uncertainty and fumblings,*
> *use its pages to change me.*
> *May the mystery of your Word*
> *always lead back to you, Jesus, the Living Word.*
> *May the word made text always take me to you,*
> *the Word made flesh.*
> *And may this Spirit-inspired Word forever*
> *guide me gently back to you,*
> *the Spirit-conceived Word.*
> *Amen.*[12]

Chat Notes

▩ God, mystery feels risky.

My parents' parties were legendary. They had a wide circle of friends and were known for their hospitality, so their annual Christmas bash was a guaranteed humdinger. One year, when I was about eight or nine years old, the date was set, the invitations were sent out, the appetizers plated, the cocktails waiting to be shaken not stirred, and the house and us kids scrubbed and ready for guests. Even Mum's lipstick glistened festively in the Christmas lights. Everything was perfect. Except for the downstairs loo.

At the time, our house was halfway through a renovation. The seventies avocado green powder room fixtures had been replaced with bright white ones, but the walls—Edwardian plaster lined with fresh brown lining paper—were yet to be painted. Determined to turn their half-finished facilities into a memorable party favorite, my innovative parents provided markers, paints, and pastels, and invited guests to be creative and decorate the walls with "pretty graffiti."

As the night wore on and the guests were fueled by good food, friends, and wine, the graffiti grew bolder, wittier, and occasionally more risqué. The following morning, having been banished to bed before things got interesting, I tiptoed downstairs to inspect the evening's collective "art." There were clever doodles, *New Yorker*–worthy cartoons, knock-knock jokes, and the occasional political rant, but one particular line stood out and has stuck with me since:

"I used to be indecisive, but now I'm not so sure."

Lord, sitting here today as I wrestle with so much of my faith, I find myself nodding along sagely with the author of that loo wall graffiti. I long for their apparent ease in the not knowing, but I simultaneously worry this place of mystery— maybe even of indecision—is a cop-out. God, mystery sure feels high-risk.

With the church becoming increasingly vocal and divisive on no small number of topics, many of us feel a pressure to know with certainty what we believe, where we stand, and why. Whether we're around Thanksgiving dinner, on the bleachers at our kid's lacrosse game, or in our Bible study group, the issues feel bigger and our decisions about where we stand feel weightier and more pressing than ever before.

If you're from a theologically more conservative background, living with more mystery and less certainty can feel as if you're not taking a stand on the gospel. You might be accused of becoming too liberal, going soft, letting the world warp your views and faith, deconstructing, losing your faith, or worse, letting God down.

You might worry you're what James called "double-minded and unstable" and "like a wave of the sea, blown and tossed by the wind" (James 1:6–8).

Do we have to have answers? Can we live in uncertainty if we call it mystery? Where are you, God, in our bewilderment and not knowing?

Great questions. Let's chat with God.

God, Can We Chat?

Consider the Facts

What specific incident(s) has caused you to ask this question? (Just the facts, ma'am!)

- Was there a time when most of what you believed about GodFaithChurch was clear? If so, what helped you to feel that way?

- If you've always been unsure of what to think, why do you think this question has bubbled to the surface now? What, if anything, has changed?

Honor the Story You're Telling Yourself

Get curious about your emotions and inner narrative around this question. In the following exercises, use this prompt: *The story I'm telling myself is . . .*

- How does the idea sit with you that you might never find clarity on some of the issues you're struggling with?

- What potential risks do you see of living with a greater level of mystery and of not knowing in your faith?

- What's your relationship like with God when you don't know what to believe?

Ask God What He Has to Say

Prayerfully ask God to show you how he sees things, including you, and what he might want to say to you as a friend today.

- If you and God went for a walk together and you confessed how you don't know what to believe anymore, told him how that makes you feel, and dared to tell him the stories running through your mind about him and yourself, what do you think he would say?

- You're not the only one who doesn't know what to believe, so take a moment and ask God to show you how he feels about anyone who struggles with uncertainty.

Often it's easier to hear God's heart for someone else than for ourselves, as we can assume that we're the exception.

Team Up with God Moving Forward

As you walk through daily life and face its inevitable frustrations, questions, and doubts, how can you intentionally link arms with God and doubt-walk through your unanswered questions?

- Take a moment to imagine taking all the potential risks and costs of living in greater mystery and putting them in a backpack. Then imagine Jesus doing the same with all the wonderful things about his unknowability. Now prayerfully visualize switching backpacks and asking Jesus to hold your pack and help you unpack the one he gave you.

- As you take all the positive things about God's unknowability out of the pack Jesus just gave you, is there anything surprising that you weren't expecting or something you need him to explain?

- As Jesus begins to unpack the bag you gave him, is there anything you want to say to him or explain? Are there particular issues inside you need him to carry for a while longer?

Lord, I used to know what to believe.
Now I'm not so sure.
It's all so confusing, disorienting, and frustrating.
I don't want to do the wrong thing or let
anyone down, especially you.

You're unchanging, yet everything seems different. Weightier.
May I practice your presence in my confusion.
May your mystery bring me peace, not disquiet,
feeding my soul where it longs for more.
Amen.

Chat Notes

_____

_____

_____

_____

_____

_____

_____

_____

_____

_____

Treasure Awaits

Whether you came to faith twenty minutes ago, alone and sobbing curled on your bathroom floor, or twenty years ago in a joy-filled stadium of soul-searching college kids, you've probably bumped into one of faith's many paradoxes. Like locked treasure chests laden with untold riches, these paradoxes hold the breathtaking breadth and depth of our faith and of God's mystery, yet we never get to open them fully. We see the beautiful jewels and metalwork adorning their exterior. We read the carved inscriptions on their sides and catch the fragrance of their contents through narrow slats in their ornate latticework lids, and we talk about the wonders they contain. But our humanity ensures the chests remain locked. Our limited human brains are unable to prize them open, no matter how long or how hard we try.

These paradox treasure chests are central to our Christian theology and have been hotly debated and thoroughly discussed since long before Jesus's time—just look at Ecclesiastes, Job, Psalms, and the prophets. Yet, despite our best efforts, they remain forever unopenable. Their vastness, unsolvable.

For the most part, these faith paradoxes don't bother us. In fact, we find their insolvability vaguely comforting. In their infinite depth and our inability to pin them down, we enjoy a certain security, confident that God not only created them but understands them, even if we've only managed to scratch their surface. Rather than holding our faith back or hindering our spiritual growth and formation, these paradoxes often make it easier, giving us permission to leave such weighty theological conundrums in God's capable hands.

Take, for example, the paradox of God's grace and judgment—I mean, who doesn't want a God who's both perfectly just *and* also merciful when we can't help but screw up? Or take the tension between God's absolute, divine sovereignty and our genuine freedom to choose. We get an all-powerful God *and* we get to live by our own choices. It's a win-win. Even the paradox of the Trinity—one God in three persons—isn't something we try to solve, even if we do try and explain it. Rather, we gratefully live in light of its many benefits—like having a divine support squad of love, redemption, and constant companionship rolled into one. Such matters contradict and challenge our limited (compared to God's) intelligence, yet we embrace them.

Still, there's one treasure box we find more challenging than any of the others. We continually try to pick its lock or falsely claim its precious contents have been uncovered once and for all. This is the paradox of the knowability of God's nature. In his wonderfully life-giving, deeply loving, and equally annoying, enigmatic way, God is both wholly unknowable and yet fully knowable. And for many of us, that's a problem. This dual nature of God—his profound mystery that surpasses human understanding and his willingness to reveal himself to those who seek him with sincerity and faith—is both freeing and frustrating.

The question for us all is whether we're happy to lean into its mystery. Can we embrace the unknowability of our God? Can we trust him in the uncertainty of our pain, taking our doubts and questions to him as we go, knowing we are loved in a way we'll never grasp? Are we willing to do all we can to know the knowable parts of our God, while simultaneously abandoning our relentless quest to grasp the unknowable?

Or will we fight for the right to be certain? Will we continually limit the growth of our faith and the closeness of our relationship with God by claiming we need answers? And will we insist on understanding God's ways, God's Word, and the church before we can trust or keep going?

Living in mystery can be fun and frustrating, life-giving and draining, faith-building and faith-zapping—often all at once. But let's not forget we still have a choice. Letting go of our need for certainty is more than just a decision about how we think; it's a decision about how we live.[13]

After all my doubting and screaming, chatting and praying, reading and interrogating, I'm no closer to certainty than I was before my faith started to unravel. I have fewer answers, more questions, and an unfolding realization that this is never going to change. But one thing's for sure—I'm closer to God than I've ever been.

> **Doubt has given my faith a new lease on life just when I thought it was fading.**

Discovering that we can be simultaneously lost and found, certain and uncertain, trusting and skeptical, faith-filled and faith-drained, believing and doubting, and a hundred other mysterious paradoxes has set my faith free more than anything else since the day I said, "Yes, Jesus, I'd love to be your friend. Thanks." Doubt has given my faith a new lease on life just when I thought it was fading. The question I've decided to say a resounding "yes" to is this: *Am I willing to trade certainty in God for intimacy with him?* My question to you is the same.

But why, Niki? I hear you ask. *Why do I need to trade? Can't I have both?*

Unfortunately not. Certainty is unobtainable. Yes, we can feel certain in our beliefs, but not in knowing God's ways, thinking, and nature. And if we're not careful—as I've discovered to my faith's detriment—our constant quest for certainty can eventually rob us of our closeness with God. Giving up that quest is an act of spiritual survival.

Increasingly we hear the world telling us to "discover your truth" and "live your truth." At the same time, prominent faith leaders fight back and tell us there's only one truth, and if we are to be true believers we must know it, believe it, and live it. But everything in me wants to scream, "I hear you, and I want to. But I can't! I have too many unanswerable questions!" Trading certainty for mystery has, quite honestly, been a relief.

The peace I've discovered in my questions has taken me back to the heady days of my new faith in that Victorian church with its bare brick walls. Stripped of its plasterwork and ornate molding, our faith becomes more genuine, refreshing, and welcoming. Like Pete Greig says, we will discover how "time and time again, God ignores [our] most pressing questions in order to answer the deepest longing of [our] heart."[14]

> **When we dare to doubt, we discover that our Father, who has known and loved us all along, is waiting, his arms thrown wide in welcome.**

No one picks up a book like this if they don't love their faith. You didn't read this far because you want to throw in the towel. Quite the opposite. So let me encourage you: When we dare to doubt, we find the rest Jesus promised for the weary and heavy laden. When we dare to doubt, we discover that our Father, who has known and loved us all along, is waiting, his arms thrown wide in welcome. Finally, we can take a breath. We are wholly loved, doubts and all. We can relax, knowing our faith isn't coming apart but coming together. And we can make peace with the knowledge that on this side of heaven we'll always carry a few questions.

Augustine was right: God made us for himself, and our hearts are restless until we rest in him.[15] And for those of us who've assumed rest will come when our questions are answered, we can finally exhale.

Coming to God in our uncertainty, when nothing makes sense, is a step towards the life of abundance, freedom, and rest he longs for us to accept. It's an act of trust when trusting him is the last thing we think we can or want to do. Chatting to God in the midst of our doubts is our way of saying, "I don't get it, God, but I want to know and be with you more than I want answers. So I'm willing to be willing to show up in the mystery. Let's do this." We, like Rachel Held Evans, will be able to say, "I am a Christian because the story of Jesus is still the story I'm willing to risk being wrong about."[16]

How do we live in mystery without imploding or living life frustrated—or worse, walking away from God? How do we become comfortable holding doubt and faith together and being okay with it? How do we turn our doubts from being our faith's kryptonite to its superpower? We keep moving, keep talking, keep listening, keep staying open, curious, willing, and full of love—in relationship with God and others.

As you go, may your daring honesty with God continue. As you walk with him in the gloriously freeing and frustratingly endless mystery of faith, may your chats bring you into the untold treasures of his closeness, one doubt at a time.

Blessings for the Crossroads

May we, the believers, doubters, skeptics—
doubting believers and believing doubters—
along with the disillusioned, frustrated, and spiritually curious,
forever seek as those who will find,
and be found as those who keep seeking.

And may you who dare to doubt
know that I, along with a great cloud of witnesses—
Esther, Sarah, Miriam, Deborah, Hannah, Mary, Martha,
Julian of Norwich, Hildegard of Bingen, Susanna
Wesley, and Mother Teresa, to name but a few—
are praying and interceding on your behalf.

As you doubt in conversation with God,
may you see this as the holy work it is,
no matter how hard or frustrating.
As you gift yourself time and space to
come to the Word made flesh,
may he hug you like you've never been hugged before.

May you take joy in the wrestling, find intimacy in the not knowing,
and enjoy peace in his presence with you.
As you walk and talk with God,
may your shoulders drop and your heartbeat slow
as the fear of your faith fading loosens its grip.

May you live courageously in "the space between
who God is and what we can know of God,"
because that's where faith resides.[17]
And when you're tempted to walk away,
believing he's done with you, isn't for you,
or that answers are the only way forward,
may he strengthen you to keep talking,
encourage you to keep listening,
and above all lead you as you keep doubting—
walking through mystery together.

May you who never saw him yet love him (however shakily),
and you who still don't see him yet trust
him (however questioningly),
and you who've kept on believing (despite
everything life's thrown your way),
be filled with the inexpressible and glorious joy of receiving
what you're longing for: Your promised salvation.
Your soul's victory.

May you know, as all God's people can—
whether they're doubting believers or believing doubters—
how unfathomably wide, long, high,
and deep God's love is for you.
May you experience this love of Christ,
even though it's too mind-blowing
to wrap our brains around.
May you be filled with so much of the fullness
of life and power that comes from God,
that it overflows and pours out of you.

May you feel the joy of living loved
without the demands for certainty or answers.
May you be set free from the pressure and desire
to have your questions satisfied,
and may you know the intimacy of his mysterious love.

(Based on 1 Peter 1:8–9 and Ephesians 3:18–19)

Helpful Resources

At GodCanWeChat.com, you'll find lots of free resources, including:

- **The *God, Can We Chat?* Group Discussion Guide.** Read as a church or with your Bible study group or book club, and be guided by these helpful and insightful questions.

- **How to Hear God's Voice in a Noisy World.** Hear God's voice more confidently by tuning out the world's chatter and into what he has to say to you.

- **17 Ways to Reconnect with God When He Feels Far Off**

- **The *God, Can We Chat?* CHAT Guided Prayer Templates.** Make this prayer practice your own and use it with any question or issue you'd like to take to God.

- **Letters from the Bible.** More letters from our friends in the Bible that didn't make it into the book!

Go to GodCanWeChat.com.

Thanks! You're the Best

Writing is a team sport, and putting a book into the world isn't for sissies. Which means this sissy couldn't have done it without you all. (Or should I say y'all?) Thank you to . . .

Al, for everything. LTD with you and God is my happy place. Let's never stop adventuring.

J, Soph, and Ems, you make everything worth it (Eph. 3:14–19).

Rachel Jacobson, for taking a chance on me.

Kelsey Bowen, for never doubting me or this book on doubt. Because of you, I'm a better writer.

Amy Nemecek, for navigating the editing roller coaster with humor and grace.

Eileen Hanson and the Revell team, for another great launch.

My OMM (Kathy, Trina, Nicole), for not letting me quit, being my safe place, and cheering me on.

My Ablaze friends, for helping me discern God's heart for me and this book, and for so much more.

Becky and Jill, for sharing your stories so candidly. And Tom, for nailing the heart of doubt's issues!

Friends (you know who you are), for putting up with grumpy, absent, book-writing Niki, and for celebrating small wins along the way.

And you, dear reader, for honestly sharing your questions, pain, and stories. For trusting me with your longings and fears. For not giving up on your faith or on God. You won't regret it.

Finding words for my deep gratitude has silenced me. A rare occurrence indeed!

Notes

Before You Dive In

1. Marie Forleo, Facebook post, October 20, 2012, https://www.facebook
.com/marieforleo/posts/clarity-comes-from-engagement-not-thought-take
-action-now-youll-find-your-truth/10151124690403978/.

Part 1 God, I'm Lost

1. John Newton, "Amazing Grace," public domain, accessed July 22, 2024,
https://hymnary.org/text/amazing_grace_how_sweet_the_sound.

2. Barbara Kingsolver, *Demon Copperhead* (Harper, 2022), 9.

3. Rachel Held Evans, *Inspired: Slaying Giants, Walking on Water, and
Loving the Bible Again* (Thomas Nelson, 2018), 164.

4. For more on this, visit AmbiguousLoss.com.

5. Joe Terrell, "Five Real Reasons Young People Are Deconstructing Christianity," CareyNieuwhof.com, accessed June 13, 2024, https://careynieuwhof
.com/five-real-reasons-young-people-are-deconstructing-their-faith/.

6. Evans, *Inspired*, 25.

7. Evans, *Inspired*, 25.

8. Parker J. Palmer, *Let Your Life Speak: The Voice of Vocation* (Jossey-
Bass, 1999), 3.

9. *Merriam-Webster Dictionary*, "doubt," accessed July 24, 2024, https://
www.merriam-webster.com/thesaurus/doubt.

10. Eugene H. Peterson, *The Message: The Bible in Contemporary Language* (NavPress, 2005), 839.

11. Peterson, *The Message*, 839.

12. Julian of Norwich, *Revelations of Divine Love* (Oxford University
Press, 2015), 75.

13. Pierre Teilhard de Chardin, "Patient Trust," IgnatianSpirituality.com, accessed July 15, 2024, https://www.ignatianspirituality.com/prayer-of-theil hard-de-chardin/.

14. Barbara Brown Taylor wrote a book titled *Holy Envy* (HarperOne, 2019) in which she discusses this at length. To learn more, see "Make Room for 'Holy Envy' When Learning About Other Faiths," U.S. Catholic, August 20, 2019, https://uscatholic.org/articles/201908/learning-about-other-faiths -make-room-for-holy-envy-says-this-episcopal-priest/.

Part 2 God, Is This True?

1. Emily P. Freeman, "The Power of Naming," *The Next Right Thing Podcast*, episode 6, accessed July 15, 2024, https://emilypfreeman.com/podcast /06-know-the-power-of-naming/.

2. "Psalm 139:23–24," YouVersion, accessed October 12, 2024, https:// www.bible.com/videos/45110-psalm-139-23-24.

3. Henri Poincaré, *The Value of Science: Essential Writings of Henri Poincaré* (Modern Library, 2001), 4.

4. If you want a mathematical explanation, you can find one at https://en .wikipedia.org/wiki/Three_cups_problem.

5. Evans, *Inspired*, 68.

6. Jennifer Dukes Lee, *Stuff I'd Only Tell God: A Guided Journal of Courageous Honesty, Obsessive Truth-Telling, and Beautifully Ruthless Self Discovery* (Bethany House, 2023), 8.

7. "CH₃COOH," *Lessons in Chemistry*, season 1, episode 5 (Aggregate Films/Apple Studios, 2023).

8. Peter Enns, *The Sin of Certainty: Why God Desires Our Trust More Than Our "Correct" Beliefs* (HarperOne, 2016), 5.

Part 3 God, Can We Chat?

1. Pete Greig, *How to Pray: A Simple Guide for Normal People* (NavPress, 2019), xvii.

2. If you're unfamiliar with CBT and would like a more detailed explanation, see the helpful article "What Is CBT?," PsychologyTools.com, https:// www.psychologytools.com/self-help/what-is-cbt/. If you're after a deep dive into CBT and want a respected book, I'd recommend Judith S. Beck's, *Cognitive Behavior Therapy: Basics and Beyond* (Guilford Press, 2011).

3. "What Story Am I Telling Myself and What Impact Is That Having on My Feelings and Actions?," *Hustle + Hush*, March 20, 2020, https://www .hustleandhush.com/blog/2020/3/20/what-story-am-i-telling-myself-and -what-impact-is-that-having-on-my-feelings-and-actions.

4. Rami Shapiro, "Preface," in *Hasidic Tales* (SkyLight Paths, 2004), xviii.

5. Dan Piraro, *Bizarro* (cartoon), January 26, 2007, Comics Kingdom, https://comicskingdom.com/bizarro/2007-01-26.

6. Carey Nieuwhof, "3 Things Christians Do That Non-Christians Despise," Carey Nieuwhof, accessed June 22, 2024, https://careynieuwhof.com/3-things-christians-do-that-non-christians-despise/.

7. Donavyn Coffey, "Why Does Christianity Have So Many Denominations?," LiveScience, last updated July 29, 2022, https://www.livescience.com/christianity-denominations.html.

8. Edward Abbey, *The Fool's Progress: An Honest Novel* (Macmillan, 1998), 14.

9. "What Are Anxiety Disorders?," American Psychiatric Association, accessed June 14, 2024, https://www.psychiatry.org/patients-families/anxiety-disorders/what-are-anxiety-disorders.

10. C. S. Lewis, *A Grief Observed* (Bantam Books, 1976), 5.

11. Frank Newport, "Fewer in U.S. Now See Bible as Literal Word of God," Gallup, July 6, 2022, https://news.gallup.com/poll/394262/fewer-bible-literal-word-god.aspx.

12. Inspired by Derek Vreeland, "Why Biblical Inerrancy Doesn't Work," Missio Alliance, April 12, 2019, https://www.missioalliance.org/why-biblical-inerrancy-doesnt-work/.

13. Enns, *The Sin of Certainty*, 204.

14. Pete Greig, *Dirty Glory: Go Where Your Best Prayers Take You* (Tyndale, 2016), 56.

15. Augustine, *Confessions*, book 1, chapter 1.

16. Evans, *Inspired*, 164.

17. Kirsten Sanders, "Wait, You're Not Deconstructing?," *Christianity Today*, February 14, 2022, https://www.christianitytoday.com/ct/2022/march/exvangelical-theology-wait-youre-not-deconstructing.html.

NIKI HARDY is the author of the Audi Award–nominated *Breathe Again: How to Live Well When Life Falls Apart* and *One Minute Prayers for Women with Cancer*, and has been featured on the Hallmark Channel, Life Today, and Premier Radio. Having left corporate life, been to seminary, moved continents, planted churches, started businesses and nonprofits, and navigated loss, cancer, church hurt, and painful uncertainty, she firmly believes God loves a cheerful doubter. Niki lives in North Carolina with her husband and ridiculous Doodle, Charlie, who is the main reason their three grown kids come home. Learn more at NikiHardy.com.